*Assessing
the President*

Assessing the President

THE MEDIA, ELITE OPINION, AND PUBLIC SUPPORT

Richard A. Brody

STANFORD UNIVERSITY PRESS

Stanford, California 1991

Stanford University Press
Stanford, California

© 1991 by the Board of Trustees of the
Leland Stanford Junior University

Printed in the United States of America

Original printing 1991

Last figure below indicates year of this printing:
01 00 99 98 97 96 95 94 93 92

CIP data are at the end of the book

For Marjorie, Gordon, David, and Aaron
with more love than I can express

Acknowledgments

ACROSS THE TWO DECADES that it took to bring this study to completion, I have incurred many debts to institutions and individuals. The Center for Advanced Study in the Behavioral Sciences was the place where the idea was conceived and the first paper written; that was in 1967–68. Thirteen years later, the Government Department of the London School of Economics and Political Science, especially Bill Letwin and Ken Minogue, helped the project along by giving me a faculty visitorship and good company. Stanford University has assisted me in dozens of ways. The American Enterprise Institute for Public Policy Research gave me a grant to continue the project, Austin Ranney and Howard Penniman being instrumental in this respect.

I have profited enormously from long interviews and conversations with working journalists. I am especially grateful to Leonard Downie, Jr., of the Washington *Post*, Peter Jennings of ABC-TV News, Robert Siegel of NPR, Rick Smith of the New York *Times*, Clark Hoyt of Knight-Ridder, Evans Witt of AP, and John Jacobs of the San Francisco *Examiner*. Academic colleagues have been no less helpful. Paul Sniderman, Ray Wolfinger, J. Merrill Shanks, Nelson Polsby, Aaron Wildavsky, Sam Kernell, Gary Jacobson, Geoff Garrett, George Tsebelis, and John Ferejohn have listened patiently, commented critically, and above all endured my enthusiasm. That's friendship!

But I have had more than informants and commentators over these years, I have had collaborators, too. At various stages of this project, I have worked alongside Phil Stone, Ben Page, David Segre, Tim Haight, William Lowry, Robert Griffin, Elizabeth Economy, and Catherine Shapiro. The learning that took place in those collaborations is reflected in the pages that follow. In collaborative work it is impossible to pin down the source of good ideas; the bad ideas that remain are mine, all mine.

R.A.B.

Contents

PART I: *Introduction*   3

1. The American People and Presidential Popularity   7

2. The Presidential Honeymoon   27

3. The Rally Phenomenon in Public Opinion   45

PART II: *Presidential Popularity After
the Honeymoon*   81

4. Of Time and Presidential Popularity   83

5. Economic Performance and Presidential Popularity   91

6. Daily News and the Dynamics of Support
for the President   104

7. Daily News and Public Support for the President,
Kennedy Through Ford   133

8. Daily News and Public Support for Presidents Carter and Reagan   146

9. Public Support for the President and Democratic Control of Public Policy   168

References Cited   179
Index   189

Introduction

Introduction

THE STANDING OF the president with the American people has come to have a political life of its own. A president's "popularity" is said to be a political resource that can help him achieve his program, keep challengers at bay, and guide his and other political leaders' expectations about the president's party's prospects in presidential and congressional elections. A political fact with consequences as important as these will be attended to by political elites and is worthy of our close attention.

"Popularity" is the most frequently used and utterly confusing of many synonyms for the public's evaluation of the job performance of the incumbent president. It is confusing because it connotes image rather than substance and surface rather than depth. If the Gallup Poll is to be believed, all presidents are "admired" by the American people and are in that sense "popular." This admiration is relatively invariant over time and across administrations. By contrast the public's evaluation of the way in which the incumbent president is handling "his job as president" is invariant neither within nor between administrations.

"Popularity" in the sense of "admiration" is not a political resource. How could it be? It responds to nothing that politicians and the public care deeply about. President Nixon was still widely "admired" on the eve of his resignation. But of course his administration and his capacity to lead the American polity were a shambles. His performance ratings reflected the shattered state of his presidency; his "admiration" score did not.

"Popularity" as a performance rating is a political resource; it is this evaluation which is the subject of this extended essay. The central claim of the book is that the American people form and revise their impressions of the quality of presidential performance on evidence contained in reports of politics and policy outcomes—political news—in the news media. Since the public is not always certain what news implies about the success or failure of policy, it often takes its guidance on the meaning of the news from political opinion leaders. The president, other elected officials, respected members of the press, and a handful of other commentators who have earned the trust of at least a segment of the public affect opinion by interpreting events that are unclear in their political meaning. The news carries these interpretations to the public along with the details of the events themselves.

This process, which will be described at length and explored in this book, is not innocent of politics. The interpretations placed on events by opinion leaders are politically motivated. The reactions of members of the public to the events and to the interpreters of events are guided by political predispositions such as partisanship, ideology, and political attitudes such as cynicism, respect, and trust. In a word, the process of opinion formation is "politicized."

In its emphases on the role of the media, opinion leadership, and the politics of the opinion formation process, this study departs to some degree from previous work on presidential popularity. This departure is especially evident when considering previous models of the process that emphasize reflexive responses on the part of the public to such events as the election of the president and international crises, or simply to the passage of time. There is no gainsaying the debt this study owes to these earlier models—they serve as an important stimulus for this enterprise—but the version of the process essayed in this book aims at a theory of public opinion that is faithful to what we know about the capacities of the public, the practices of the media, and the motives of the political elite.

The study begins with a detailed justification for paying strict attention to the sources of the public's evaluation of the president. It also suggests that both episodic and inertial factors affect the ebb and flow of public support for the president. The balance of the book is concerned with illuminating these short-term and long-term sources of support. Chapters Two and Three, respectively, examine "special moments"—the "honeymoon" at the beginning of a presidential term and the "rally" of presidential support that accompanies international crises. These two kinds of episodes are viewed as the principal interruptions to the ebbs and flows of support that normally constitute the dynamic of public evaluation of the president; here it is the mix of information that is treated as unusual— the public is treated as reacting as expected to the information it receives. Chapters Four, Five, and Six consider various explanations of inertial patterns of support. Tests of the "opinion leadership" model, which is developed in Chapter Six, are carried out in Chapters Seven and Eight. Chapter Nine looks at the wider implications of the book's findings. We begin in Chapter One with the public opinion history of our most recent presidents.

CHAPTER I

The American People and Presidential Popularity

THROUGH THE SUMMER OF 1990, events had been kind to George Bush. During his first year in office, apart from the brutal reversal of the trend toward a more open society in China, President Bush got everything he could have wished for and more from a rapidly changing world.

Beginning in June 1989 the media brought to the American people news reports of events that have markedly changed the problems faced by U.S. policymakers. The most obvious of these changes are (1) the complete unraveling of the fabric of Soviet alliances in Eastern Europe and its reverberations within NATO and the Federal Republic of Germany in particular; (2) the surfacing of deep and bitter strains within the Soviet Union itself that have redirected Soviet energies inward and brought into the open the massive problems of the Soviet economy; (3) the beginning of profound changes in the structure of South African society and continued progress in the democratization of Latin American nations—which manifested itself in the peaceful removal of Daniel Ortega from power in Nicaragua. In a more active mode, our direct intervention in Panama achieved the overthrow of the Noriega government.

The good news during President Bush's first year in office
was not exclusively in the realm of foreign policy: inflation and
unemployment remained in check and the frequently predicted
economic downturn did not materialize.

However positive the news compressed into this capsule
year-in-review, we should not lose sight of the fact that profound domestic and foreign policy problems remain and are
regularly brought to the American public's attention—drugs,
AIDS, poverty, the insecurity of savings and loan associations,
and conflict in the Middle East come easily to mind. Further,
there is no denying that events which appeared as good news
during President Bush's first year have already created new
problems for American public policy—consider, for example, a
reunited Germany and the future of NATO, the balancing of
claims for scarce foreign aid funds between present recipients
and the new democracies in Eastern Europe and Central America, the reemergence of virulent forms of nationalism and eth-
nic strife in the Soviet Union and Eastern Europe, and the increase in emigration from the Soviet Union to Israel.

We certainly should not lose sight of the fact that problem-
solvers will not be idle during the remainder of the Bush presidency, but neither should we ignore the fact that during President Bush's first year in office, unlike many periods of recent
American history, the persistent and emerging problems have
had to compete for headline space with an extraordinary volume of very positive news. More often than not while headlines proclaimed the dramatic positive news, news of unsolved
problems was relegated to the back pages of the paper and the
tag end of the television news broadcast.

Even without detailed investigation it is not difficult to
characterize the responses of American opinion leadership to
the headline events of the first eighteen-odd months of the
Bush presidency. The bloody repression in Beijing produced
uniformly negative expressions of shock, disappointment, and
outrage among American political leaders in both parties and
all ideological camps. However, criticism of President Bush's

China policy did not emerge until the beginning of the political battles over the provision of sanctuary for Chinese students in the United States. The elections in Poland, the breaching of the Berlin Wall, Lithuania's declaration of independence, the moves of Romania, Bulgaria, Hungary, Czechoslovakia, and East Germany away from communism and Soviet domination all engendered positively joyful comments from political leaders. The Cold War was over and the West had won. Why would any politician quarrel with such success?

Panama was a different story. It began with heated partisan dispute among opinion leaders over the introduction of American troops, but the critics fell silent after General Noriega was in custody and President Bush announced that the "four objectives" of the intervention had been accomplished and that American troops were being withdrawn.

What does all this have to do with public support for the president? It is the central claim of this book that the American people form and revise their collective evaluation of the president on the evidence of policy success and failure contained in daily news reports in the mass media. In Chapter Six the why and wherefore of this process will be laid out in detail. For our present purposes it is sufficient to state that the events themselves are the dynamic ingredients of the processes of opinion formation and change. Insofar as the significance of the events is appreciated by a major portion of the American people, their effect on public evaluation of the president will depend primarily on the content of news stories, as such. However, insofar as the significance of an event is not apparent to the public, its meaning will be supplied by the reactions to the events and the interpretations of them offered by opinion leaders. These reactions and interpretations are also, by and large, carried to the public by the media. All of this, of course, means that factors which affect the content of news stories also affect the evaluation of the president. It implies that factors predisposing the public to credit or discount the reactions and interpretations of opinion leaders also affect changes in public support. And it also implies that anything which motivates the reactions and interpretations of opinion leaders is a part of the evaluation dynamic as well.

Events have been kind to President Bush in the eighteen-odd month since he took office; the news has been extraordinarily good; and the American people have responded accordingly. The Gallup Poll measure of public support for the president—namely, the percent "approving" of the way the president is "handling his job"—shows that President Bush has had a high level of support from the American people ever since his inauguration. The trend in this measure is reported in Figure 1.1.

Setting aside for the moment the period January through May 1989, the substantial increase in support for President Bush between May 1989 and February 1990 is readily apparent. The trend in President Bush's job approval rating is unusual. This can be seen by comparing his approval ratings with the ratings of Presidents Carter and Reagan during the same period in their presidencies; this comparison is presented in Figure 1.2.

From the polls taken immediately after inauguration and

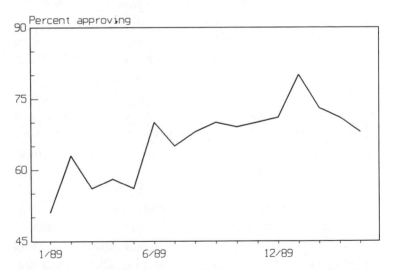

Figure 1.1. Public Approval of President Bush. SOURCE. Gallup Opinion Index.

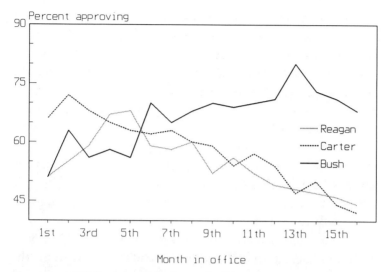

Figure 1.2. Public Approval of Presidents Bush, Carter, and Reagan.
SOURCE. Gallup Opinion Indexes.

for the next five months the differences between the trends for these three presidents are not especially remarkable. However, starting in the sixth month of the first year of these three presidencies the trends diverge. Consistent with the remarkable volume of good news reaching the American people, President Bush's approval ratings increased. Faced with news of a different sort, Presidents Carter and Reagan lost support.

We cannot know how events will treat George Bush during the balance of his presidency, but we can increase our understanding of the ways in which information affects the public's judgment of presidents in general. We do not yet know how his remarkable level of support will affect the politics of President Bush's relations with other parts of the American polity, but we can try to understand how this has worked out in the past. It is with the recent past that we begin our search for understanding.

On the sixth of November, 1980, nearly 60 percent of those Americans who went to the polls voted to deny President Carter a second term. Even among the 41 percent who preferred him to the other candidates we find a great many who "disapproved" of the way he was "handling his job as president."[1] The polls taken at the time of the election are not the first indication we have that the public was unhappy with the way President Carter was doing his job: thirty months after he had taken the oath of office, fewer than one American in three was willing to report that on balance he or she "approved" of the way President Carter was "handling his job as president."[2] In the nine Gallup surveys done from June through October 1979—the period in which Senator Kennedy was making a final decision on whether to challenge President Carter's renomination—the president's approval rating averaged only 30 percent. But the worst was yet to come: a year later, in July of 1980, when his reelection campaign was beginning to take shape and just prior to his victory at the Democratic National Convention, the proportion of the public approving of the Carter performance dropped to 21 percent, the lowest rating of any incumbent recorded by the Gallup Poll. By any standard, these figures depict a thoroughgoing rejection of President Carter's performance as the figure who dominated the formation of American public policy. Yet President Carter did not face a dissatisfied public throughout his time in office; if his presidency ended with mass rejection, it began with a fund of public hope and support. Despite the narrowness of his victory over President Ford, President Carter began his term with the approval of over 80 percent of those who had formed an impression of his performance.[3] The fact that President Carter's rating during this "honeymoon" period (of which we will have more to say below) did not much differ from those of other postwar American

1. The CPS/NES survey in the fall of 1980 indicated that Carter voters were split 74 to 26 approve/disapprove on his job performance. Of course, those who voted against him were more likely to express dissatisfaction with his handling of the job; among this group, we find a 14 to 86 split.

2. American Institute of Public Opinion Research [hereafter AIPO or Gallup Poll], Poll # 1132G (6/29–7/2/79).

3. The average "approval" figure for those with an opinion, in the fourteen Gallup Polls in the first six months of the Carter presidency, is 81.8 percent. If we take into account those who express no opinion of his performance, President Carter's average approval rating over this period was 66.6 percent.

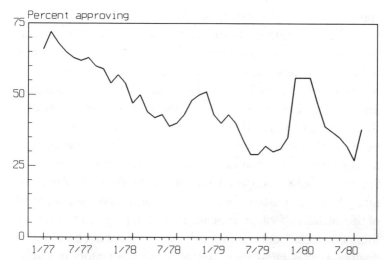

Figure 1.3. Public Approval of President Carter. SOURCE. Gallup Opinion Index.

presidents does not gainsay the fact that he was showing the American public the kind of performance it expected and to which it responded positively.

But the honeymoon was to be short lived: if we view in detail the monthly approval figures over the full four years of the Carter presidency (Figure 1.3), we see how unique was his first six months. In the autumn of 1977 public approval began a steady decline and fell into the range of 50–55 percent. Despite two distinct spurts in support—in the fall of 1978 and again in the late autumn of 1979—President Carter was never again to find as many as six Americans in ten responding positively to his handling of the presidency.

We should take notice of the two upwellings of support in Figure 1.3. The first of these followed the Camp David summit meeting, which brought together President Carter, President Sadat of Egypt, and Premier Begin of Israel. The second came in the wake of the occupation of the United States Embassy in Iran. Both of these reversals of the downward trend in approval ran out of steam. Following them the rate of decline in support appears to have accelerated, but in fact, approval dropped at exactly the same rate in the eleven months after Camp David as it had in the twelve months preceding the summit.[4] The period following the onset of the hostage crisis is different: two and a half months after the hostages were taken, approval began once again to decline. Now, however, the pace was much swifter than before. Over the first thirty months of the term, the drop in approval averaged just over one percentage point per month; for the eight months after the peak of the hostage crisis rally, President Carter's support declined at three times the pre-crisis rate. Over the course of the election year, on average, approval of the president's job performance was dropping at a precipitate four percentage points per month. Approval did not continue to decline at this rate—there are equilibrating factors in public opinion (Kernell 1978)—but the new level established in the fall of 1980 (about one-in-three approving) did little to help the president's reelection bid.

It is instructive to contrast the pattern of public opinion on President Carter's performance with opinion of President Reagan during his first term (Figure 1.4). The two patterns are remarkably similar for the first two years. It is noteworthy that although President Reagan is a Republican and, therefore, a member of the minority party, his support scores after the first three months show none of the expected partisan deficit. The trend line shows the "honeymoon" plateau during the early months; President Reagan steadily lost support over the next twenty months, and then the pattern changes. Twenty-five months into his first presidential term, President Reagan's approval ratings bottomed out. Over the next eleven months fifteen percentage points were gradually added to his level of approval, and he finished his first term with more than half of the public responding positively to his job performance.

4. For the twelve months after the six-month honeymoon at the start of his term, President Carter's approval rating was dropping at an average 1.98 percentage points per month. After Camp David, for the next eleven months he lost support at the rate of 1.97 percentage points per month.

Figure 1.4. Public Approval of President Reagan. SOURCE. Gallup Opinion Index.

What did President Carter do wrong that Reagan did right? Could Carter have changed his pattern of performance evaluation and taken more support into the 1980 election? What caused the decline in Carter's support and what is the source of the sudden upturns? These are the kinds of questions that this study will attempt to answer.

It is self-evident that a candidate for reelection would be concerned about his standing with the public and the factors that affect it. But why should we, as scholars and citizens, care about a measure of public opinion like this one? We will care if we believe that it has consequences for the shape of American public policy—consequences that go beyond electoral politics as such. If the president's standing with the American people has policy consequences, then we should share the president's curiosity about the causes of fluctuations in its level. Before attempting to satisfy this curiosity, it is worth considering in what ways public evaluation of the president can be said to have policy-relevance.

Public Opinion and the Presidency

No well-informed observer would take seriously the proposition that the president is a slave to public opinion. Nor is there any reason why he should be. The president and his party are electorally accountable for his performance. But the coupling between performance evaluation and the vote is sufficiently loose to give him a great deal of latitude for policy choice.[5] Presidents and their parties cannot ignore public response to policy performance, but they need not live in fear of it. In any case, the vote is a decision based upon a comparison between the candidates (Kelley & Mirer 1974; Brody & Page 1973). An incumbent whose job performance was responded to negatively by a large number of voters could still be more appealing than the opposition candidate to enough voters to win reelection. Mass opinion on the president's job performance is only one factor in the voter's voting decision. Because it is only one factor, it provides a forecast of the electoral outcome that has only limited utility.

Mass opinion is not much of an aid to those involved in the policy process either: the public thinks about most policy problems at a level of generality that constrains the selection among detailed policy options only in the loosest degree—if at all. While this is generally true of public opinion on public policy (see Page, Shapiro & Dempsey 1986), it is doubly true of the ratings of presidential performance. The stimulus is vague and general in the extreme.[6] The response cannot contain any specific mandate for the president to follow a particular line of policy and exclude other potential policy options.

5. Sigelman (1979) reports a strong association between the incumbent's level of approval on the last pre-election poll—often six months or more before the election—and his share of the popular vote in the general election.

6. The question the Gallup Poll has asked fairly consistently since 1938 is "Do you approve or disapprove of the way President [name of the incumbent] has handled his job as president?" The CBS/New York *Times* Poll and the National Election Study ask an identical question. For a discussion of this and related survey items, see Orren (1978: 35) and Crespi (1980).

If we require that an expression of public opinion relate directly and simply to either electoral choice or policy prescription, we are not going to be much concerned about the causes of presidential popularity ratings. But direct and simple connections are not prerequisites for political consequences, and it is these consequences that command our attention.

Mass opinion of presidential performance has become an important political datum in and of itself. We recognize it as a fact that enters into the calculations that political figures make. We have, as it were, gone to school on Richard Neustadt's insight about the connection between a president's standing with the mass public and his ability to exercise influence generally throughout the government (Neustadt 1980). By this insight, mass evaluations of the president weight in the balance of power between governmental units and make political life easier or more difficult for the president than it would otherwise be.

Neustadt's argument reflects a change in the status of public opinion in political philosophy. The hypothesized links between the mass public, political leadership, and public policy underwent a transformation with Walter Lippmann's essays on public opinion. Prior to Lippmann, democratic theory held by implication if not explicitly that democratic leaders should directly translate the views of the mass public into public policy. The dominance of this view is attested to, for example, by Edmund Burke's insistence to the contrary that representatives should accord their own best judgment priority over mass opinion and by John C. Calhoun's insistence upon the legitimacy of minority opinion in the formation of public policy. Neither Burke's nor Calhoun's "correctives" make any sense if we do not assume that others were taking as given the assumption that public policy should directly reflect the opinions of majorities of mass publics.

Compared with this active role for mass opinion, public opinion is now accorded a much more passive role. Under contemporary democratic theory citizens form a mass audience before whom the drama of politics is played (Schattschneider 1960). The drama is played only partly for the public's benefit: the public is not expected to pay very close attention, but there is an abiding interest in its reaction to what is going on. Democratic politics is modeled as a conflict of organized interests vying for control of the means of satisfying those interests; public support is considered a resource in the struggle for control. Under this model, mass audience support is courted by conflicting elites for the legitimacy it confers upon their respective policy proposals and for the indications of electoral threat or comfort it provides. These indications are of interest to elites who base their right to lead upon their periodic reconfirmation by the public.

Because it is a resource over which there is competition and because it is a source of valued information, the determination of public opinion is an important activity for political elites. A variety of techniques for "measuring" public opinion are available and employed by the elite. When political leaders are trying to determine their own standing with the public upon whom their political future depends—their direct constituents—they are likely to rely upon the perceptions of intimate informants (Fenno 1978). These perceptions appear to be preferred to less personal, more formal, sources, such as opinion polls. The preference for information from political intimates may reflect some distrust of polling. But more to the point, it reflects the fact that detailed information on the likely division of the constituency on policy options facing leadership is not often found in the results of polls. Political leaders, consciously or by instinct, appear willing to trade the reliability and validity of formal polls for the depth and texture of information about constituency opinion that comes from their circle of intimate political contacts. They have to know where they stand with the public and where the public stands on the issues being decided, and they prefer this means of finding out.

Knowing one's own standing with the public is vitally important to a political leader, but knowing how the public views other political leaders is crucial as well. Under the right circumstances, the elite preference for assessment about their own standing drawn from political intimates would find expression in this context as well. However, for most of the political leaders about whom a given political leader would want to know, the proper circumstances do not obtain. Under the usual circumstance, in a nation as large and politically complex as the United States, opinion polls become the only practicable means for one leader to find out how another leader is viewed by the public. The president is the figure about whom other national leaders regularly need information, and the polls on the division of opinion in the public, on the way the president is doing his job, regularly provide this information.

The incumbent president's standing with the public appears to be related to the ease or difficulty with which he wins renomination for another term in office. This would suggest that leading figures within the president's own party look to this measure for indications of the prudence of making a serious challenge. Both Presidents Truman and Johnson dropped their bids for renomination in the wake of Gallup Poll reports that public disapproval had reached record heights. This evidence of widespread public disapproval coupled with disappointing results in their respective New Hampshire primaries—in 1952 and 1968—gave these presidents ample reason to question the likelihood of being reelected if they won renomination.

The Reagan challenge to President Ford in 1976 and the Kennedy challenge to President Carter in 1980 were mounted at a time when both incumbents' approval ratings stood well below 55 percent. That these challenges proved unsuccessful should not obscure the fact that political leaders with a great deal at stake took a major personal/political decision armed with the knowledge that the "experience of four decades indi-

TABLE I.I

Presidential Popularity and the Popular Vote

If the percent approving (A) in the last pre- election poll is	Then the incum- bent's share of the popular vote (E(v)) should be
25%	41.7%
30	43.6
35	45.5
40	47.4
45	49.3
50	51.2
55	53.1
60	55.0
65	56.9

SOURCE: Adapted from Sigelman 1979.
NOTE: See n. 7 to this chapter on the derivation of the equation $E(V) = 32.08 + .383A$.

cated that an incumbent president can generally expect a tight election if his popularity rating polls fell below the 55 percent line" ("Campaign '76": 5). A closer examination of the relationship between evaluation of job performance and the incumbent's share of the vote in his bid for reelection reveals that if an incumbent receives an approval rating, on his last preelection poll, of 47 percent or higher, he is likely to get a majority of the electoral vote.[7] However, as Table 1.1 shows, departures

7. This figure is derived from an extension of the study reported by Sigelman (1979). Sigelman regresses popular vote percentage on percent "approving" of presidential job performance in the final pre-election poll for the seven reelection bids between 1940 and 1976. The derived equation is $E(V) = 37.97 + .291A$; $R^2 = .543$; where $E(V)$ is the expected popular vote percentage of the incumbent; A is the percent approving in the final pre-election poll; and R^2 is an index (ranging from zero to one) of the strength of the relationship. With seven incumbents, this prediction equation is statistically significant. The equation is genuinely predictive within the limits of its accuracy since the final poll is generally taken months before the election. If we had used this equation to forecast the 1980 election, with President Carter's June 1980 approval rating of 32 percent, we would have expected him to get 47 ± 4 percent of the popular vote. His actual vote falls below the lower bound prediction from the Sigelman equation. We can improve Sigelman's formula by adding in the 1980 election and rederiving the equation; the new formula is $E(V) = 32.08 + .383A$; $R^2 = .722$.

upward or downward from 47 percent do not translate one-for-one into vote shares. A five-percentage-point shift leads to a 1.9 percentage point change in expected vote.

If the president's reelection looks risky, opposition within his own party is likely to grow. This opposition will be emboldened by the president's growing weakness and will be fed by and will feed the ambitions of those who feel that "four years is too long to wait, after all."

The electoral message is not the only one conveyed by the polls. Neustadt (1980) suggests that the president's task of persuading Congress that his legislative program should be passed is made easier when he enjoys widespread approval. Neustadt notwithstanding, empirical analyses of this hypothesis has produced mixed results: Edwards considers the link between passage of the president's program and his approval ratings in the public at large and in the partisan subgroups and finds that "presidential prestige does serve as a source of presidential influence in Congress" (1980: 99).

Bond and Fleisher reach the opposite conclusion. Looking at the components of the president's program and his popularity, they conclude that "the president does not win more votes nor does he receive higher levels of support when he is popular than when he is unpopular" (1982: 16).

Rivers and Rose reconcile these opposing findings: they argue that members of Congress recognize that they and the president share a common political fate "based on their understanding of how the public holds government accountable for policy failure. . . . [T]his connection promotes congressional support for the program of a popular president" (Rivers & Rose 1985: 187). However, the president's legislative program is not fixed, and when "presidential support in Congress is high [for example, when he is popular with the public], presidents tend to submit a large number of requests and to receive as a consequence lower [congressional] approval ratings" (Rivers & Rose 1985: 194).

Rivers and Rose thus show us that Bond and Fleisher's conclusion can lead to a misinterpretation of the role of public
support in the politics of a president's legislative program. A
president's rate of success in Congress may be indistinguishable when his public support is high or low, but these proportions may mask the fact that a greater number of the elements
of his program are passed when a large share of the public responds with approval to his overall policy performance.

Presidential poll ratings are important because they are
thought to be important. They are thought to be important
because political leaders look for indications of when it is safe
or dangerous to oppose their policy interests or career ambitions to those of the president and because indications of political support—which in other political contexts might be
preferred—are too limited in scope to be relied upon in this
context.

There is nothing in the Carter presidency that would disabuse us of the belief that presidential performance ratings are
politically relevant. If anything, the pattern of these ratings
and the role they are perceived to have played in his policy
problems, his fight for renomination, and his failure to be reelected have increased interest in the causes of mass evaluation
of presidential job performance. This heightened interest is fueled by a belief that things have gotten tougher for the president in two respects: it is thought that (1) people expect more
from government than they used to, and (2) presidents are
judged more harshly than they used to be when mass expectations are not met. The belief that things are now tougher for
the president also draws upon the perception that the fund of
public goodwill which permitted presidents some room to ma-
neuver—some "slack" in Robert Dahl's (1961) terminology—
and a consequent capacity to err without undue cost, has been
very nearly exhausted or indeed was put into overdraft by Vietnam, Watergate, and President Ford's pardon of Nixon. In short,
under this construction, for reasons often beyond the control of

the Carter Administration, the public lost patience with presidential performance; presidential missteps are thought to have been sufficient to set a spiral growth of disapproval in motion (Ladd 1979).

A spiral decline in presidential popularity could work as follows: after a brief "honeymoon," presidential policy missteps lead to increased public disapproval. Incremental weakness in public support strengthens the opposition of political elites. For example, it reduces the president's capacity to persuade members of Congress that support for his legislative program is withheld at their political peril. It also encourages foreign leaders to take actions that are contrary to the interests of the United States or, at least, the president's foreign policy. In turn, elite policy opposition increases presidential policy failure and, with it, increased public disappointment at the president's incapacity to fulfill expectations. This directly lowers public approval of presidential performance and sets into motion the next cycle of strengthened elite resistance, faltering presidential program, and reduced public support.

A hypersensitive system like this would be impossible to manage. Presidents are bound to make mistakes. If presidential popularity plays the role into which it is cast and if the American public is holding the president to a performance standard that is difficult (if not impossible) to achieve, the future of the president and the presidency as a source of policy leadership and as the central symbol of American politics is not at all bright. But this gloomy augury depends on the hypersensitivity of the system to presidential mistakes. Whether or not the system is or has become hypersensitive is a conclusion to be reached only after a careful consideration of the dynamics of presidential popularity. We have a number of presidencies with which to work, and a comparison of the sources of the evaluation of presidential job performance in these presidential terms should help us decide whether a change in this aspect of public opinion has taken place.

By which criteria should we make this comparison? Public opinion analysts have developed rich and varied explanations of the dynamics of presidential popularity. The analyses upon which these explanations rest range in complexity from simply labeling points on the trend line with tags indicating when notable political events took place, on the one hand, to the most esoteric multivariate statistical analyses, on the other. I will set aside the "explanations" that simply juxtapose political events and the trendline; these leave the reader with the impression that the events were in some way related to the movement of public opinion, but they are not disciplined by any systematic criteria. The "explanation" proceeds backwards; a notable departure from the public opinion trend sends the analyst off on a search for the "event" that caused it. However informative and suggestive this approach may be for a given administration, it cannot offer a basis for comparison between administrations. The bases for comparison must be comparable between presidential terms, and this requirement forces us to choose our political "events" as systematically as we can.

The available systematic explanations explicitly acknowledge that no single class of events can successfully characterize the diverse political histories of recent presidential terms of office. The analytic consequence of this recognition is that the public is modeled as responding to several types of evidence of presidential performance. A given presidential term can be compared to others on the basis of the weight the public appears to give to one type of evidence or another. What we hope to discover through these analyses is what view of the public as a collective processor of information about public policy is most consistent with the dynamics of its relative collective judgment of presidential performance. In this way we can learn about what kind of citizenry presidents face and whether the typical citizen has been changed by the political traumas of the 1960's and 1970's.

Two families of explanations have been presented by public opinion analysts. One concludes that the public acts as if what is going on, in general, and what the president does, specifically, do not much matter. Under this construction of public opinion, the public acts as if the incumbent, when he takes office, sets into motion a set of impersonal forces that act on the public's assessment of his job performance. After a brief period of suspended animation, in which the public is getting to know the new (or newly reelected) incumbent, the erosion of presidential support begins. The decline is inevitable and inexorable unless and until it is temporarily reversed by a foreign policy crisis. Put this starkly, this description of the first family of explanations is more caricature than characteristic. I will soften the starkness of the description when presenting the logic of the analysts' arguments in detail when using the approach in subsequent sections.

The second family of explanations begins with the assumption that what the president does or is thought to be doing is the key to understanding the dynamics of his popularity. The relationship between indications of the performance of the economy and public assessment of presidential proficiency has been a central focus of this model of public opinion, but it has not been the exclusive focus. Analysts working in this tradition have also employed indications of performance in foreign policy and presidential leadership in Congress to round out their explanations.

In the sections of this book that follow this introductory chapter I will examine public opinion on presidential performance from the perspective of both family traditions. We will begin simply, focusing on explanatory factors one at a time. This will appear retrograde if not downright simple-minded to those who have come to expect—justifiably in my opinion— that multivariate approaches are required when we are tackling a phenomenon as complex as the American public's response to their president. Be that as it may, the claims about what is going on here require and justify a lot of sorting out, and the best way to do this is to build upon the suggestions offered by single-factor explanations.

We will begin at the beginning of a president's term.

CHAPTER 2

The Presidential
Honeymoon

AT THE TIME OF the attempt on President Reagan's life, on March 30, 1981, two months into his presidency, there was a developing concern over his standing with the American people. Was he enjoying a honeymoon? How did his standing at this stage compare with that of previous presidents? What would be the effect of the president's standing on the prospects for his legislative package? *Newsweek* summarized the concern in an article on the politics of the president's budget: "a cloud no bigger than a pollster's printout materialized suddenly on the president's own horizon—a Gallup survey widely read in Washington—to suggest that he may not be quite the irresistible force he seemed only 60 days earlier. The news from the Gallup poll was not all bad for Reagan; his approval rating has grown from 51 percent in his first days to 59 percent now. But his score is near the record low for a president after two months in office."[1]

1. Peter Goldman et al., *Newsweek*, Mar. 30, 1981, p. 23. See also R. Evans and R. Novak, "The Honeymoon is Definitely Over," Washington *Post*, Mar. 29, 1981.

The assassination attempt did not stop the speculation or quiet the concern. Indeed, the "honeymoon" was a persistent theme of the media coverage and elite commentary that followed the shootings on the 30th of March. Once it was clear that the president was out of danger, the political effect of the events became the discussion topic. Would his program benefit from his display of personal courage? Would his popularity be affected? The president's approval rating did jump in the days immediately following the shootings at the Washington Hilton.[2]

A review of the early period of other presidencies indicates, despite the boost of support associated with the assassination attempt, that the early period of the Reagan presidency is neither unique nor even unusual. Approval of President Reagan's job performance was high and relatively stable during these months. In this respect, his first few months in office look like those of his predecessors. Why should this be the case? Why should presidents, irrespective of the size of their election victories, enjoy a respite from the falling away of public support?

The Honeymoon in Theory

The president—any president—is said to begin his term of office with a period in which the public suspends its processes of criticism and gives him a chance to get his program launched. Concepts like "early term halo," "early term surge," and "honeymoon" are used to convey the idea that presidents upon taking office enjoy an initially large positive public response. They also imply that the period is limited and that beyond it a different set of processes affect the evaluation of presidential performance.

2. Barry Sussman, "Shooting Gives Reagan Boost in Popularity," Washington *Post*, Apr. 2, 1981.

The notion of a "honeymoon" period partakes of the mystical qualities of the investment of leadership with legitimacy. By the act of taking the oath of office the person becomes *the President*. He is slightly larger than life. Not yet of Mount Rushmore proportions, perhaps, but for the time being at least a candidate for that elevated status. With his election the president enters a role that, to Americans as they are growing up, carries with it some of the inviolability derived from the mythic presentations of Washington, Jefferson, Lincoln, Wilson, and the Roosevelts. After the man becomes the president, even those who voted for the opposition feel uneasy (if not disloyal) about expressing criticism of him.

In the initial stages of a presidential term people in other parts of the political system do little to disabuse the mass public of its positive response to the new president. Because political elites follow (as well as lead) public opinion, elite criticism tends to be muted early in a presidential term. Members of Congress are waiting for the administration to get under way. Until the president puts forward his specific programs, cautious comment is the rule.

The mass media, following normal routines and practices, also tend to present a more positive picture of presidential performance early in a term than they will later on. Reporting the news (as distinguished from commenting editorially) under the norms of professional journalism requires that stories critical of presidential performance be tied to ("pegged" upon) the comments of legitimated political elites. To the extent that elite criticism is muted early in a president's term, legitimated elite commentary tends to be univocally positive. Lacking a legitimate peg upon which to hang negative comment about the president's program, the news media convey the positive message from elite to mass. To do otherwise would entail a violation of professional norms and give rise to the impression that neutrality had been exchanged for hostility toward the new administration. The desire to avoid giving this impression is reinforced by the need to establish and develop a working relationship with the members of the new administration (Grossman & Kumar 1981: 275–79).

From the perspective of the citizen attempting to evaluate the president in the first few weeks (perhaps months) of the term, information received from the American political system points to a positive judgment or at least to a suspension of negative judgment until the new administration has gotten under way. This assumes, of course, that major events do not intervene until the honeymoon period is over. The public's evaluative response is under these conditions determined (or overdetermined) by a compound of the citizens' own impulses and a lack of challenge by political elites and by the mass media. As long as the impulse-driven attitudes remain unchallenged by legitimate and valued sources of political information, we would expect the honeymoon process to continue. But it is unlikely, given the nature of the American and the international political systems, that negative comment on the president's program will be postponed for long. When it comes, information that reflects unfavorably on presidential performance can take its toll on his popularity.

The Honeymoon in Fact

The theory of presidential honeymoons makes political and social-psychological sense, but does it fit the facts? The plausibility of this theoretical sketch of the system producing public opinion during the early part of a presidential term can be explored in data from the twelve most recent presidential terms—from Eisenhower to Bush.[3] What should we expect to find in this exploration? We would expect that during the early

3. While there are three polls for the first seven months of each of Truman's terms (AIPO 1975), they are inadequate for any purpose more demanding than simple display and do not give enough data for statistical analysis.

part of the term evaluations will be untypically positive. This could mean either that the proportion of "approvers" in the public will be very high or that the decline in the proportion of "approvers" will be very slow over the honeymoon period.

Would we expect second presidential terms to enjoy the same sort of honeymoon as first terms? The only element of the model hypothesized to produce the honeymoon that is common to both the initial stages of a first presidential term and those of a second term is the fact of election itself. The president at the beginning of his second term is not a figure whose policies are unknown to the political elite, to the mass media, or to the public. Nor are his policies immune from criticism: the opposition party elite has had these policies under attack for the period of the election if not for nearly the whole of the previous four years. Within the president's own party, policy criticism has grown with the spread of primary election challenges to renomination. The incumbent has found his policies under attack by a wide spectrum of the political elite and, in consequence, the mass media have plenty of legitimate elite criticism with which to work and upon which to base their stories. Additionally, of course, the media have no need to build or develop a working relationship with the administration of a reelected incumbent since that relationship already exists. In short, knowledge and criticism of a reelected incumbent are readily available to the public.

Given the differences in the availability of information critical of the incumbent's performance, if we find that the "early term honeymoon" is a feature of both first and second terms, we will have pretty clear evidence of the potency of the mass psychological effect of election itself. But the contrary finding will be interesting as well. Judged on the basis of public evaluation of presidential performance, if the early periods of first and second terms are different from each other, we will have evidence that the citizens, who make up the mass public, work with the information they are given, and that their conclusions are reached in light of this information and their politically relevant attitudes and predispositions to judge.

Whether or not our explorations indicate that the initial stages of first and second terms are indistinguishable, we will have to decide over what period of time we expect the "honeymoon" to extend. The decision is bound to be arbitrary, but as long as it is consistently applied, it will serve the needs of our explorations. I have chosen the first seven months after inauguration as the period to consider. Seven months is long enough to give sufficient grist for our statistical mill but not so long as to require the reconstruction of the unique political history of each administration.[4]

Figures 2.1A through L display the plots of the responses to the Gallup Poll probe on presidential job performance for the first seven months of the last twelve presidential terms.

As a general proposition, first and second terms appear to be different from each other. The growing "disapproval" over the seven months tends to displace uncertainty (or a reluctance to offer an opinion) in the eight first terms and to displace approval in the four second terms. The first-term plots show relatively little trend in approval across the honeymoon period. For second terms, by this standard, there is no honeymoon; approval of presidential job performance shows no plateau in the early part of a second term.

It is easier to work with statistical summaries if we want to compare across administrations. If we regress approval percentages on month in office for the first seven months of a presidential term we can derive some very useful information. Table 2.1 summarizes the data for the early part of the Eisenhower, Johnson, Nixon, and Reagan second terms. Two measures of "approval" are presented. The first is the proportion of approv-

4. This is roughly the period after which other analysts have supposed that the "early-term" effect is exhausted. See Mueller 1973: 208–13; Kernell 1978: 573; and Haight 1978: x. Seven months gives us an average of over nine polls for each president.

ers in the total sample; the second excludes those with "no opinion" and is the proportion of those with an opinion who approve of the president's job performance. This is Stimson's measure of "relative approval" (Stimson 1976: 4).

Irrespective of which measure we choose, we are led to the conclusion that approval of job performance is not at rest during the early months of a president's second term. There is no plateau and, in this sense, there is no honeymoon period in the second term.

The data from the beginning of President Johnson's and President Reagan's second terms appear to contradict this generalization, since neither "approval" nor "relative approval" reliably trend downward across these seven months. I believe the contradiction is more apparent than real: for the first four months of his second term President Johnson's popularity was declining at over one and a half percentage points per month,[5] but the decline was halted and temporarily reversed at the time of the crisis in the Dominican Republic (April 1965) and did not resume until after the period under review was over. With so few polls in such a short time period, we cannot rule out chance as the explanation of the coincidence between the Dominican crisis and the change in the trend in evaluation of President Johnson's job performance; but it seems not too farfetched to speculate that this crisis (as many before and after it) rallied the American people behind the president (see Chapter Three below). If this was the case, the claim that second terms do not enjoy an early honeymoon would be strengthened. In the honeymoon period, the normal processes of information processing and opinion formation are supposed to be suspended. A downward drifting approval level arrested by a foreign policy crisis involving U.S. interests is a capsule description of normal

5. The regression equations covering these six polls are as follows: for expected approval, $E(App) = 72.6\% - 1.61$ (%/month), with $t_b = 2.39$; $.10 \leq P_t \leq .05$; $R^2 = .63$; for expected relative approval, $E(App_r) = 83.6\% - 2.24$ (%/month), with $t_b = 13.89$; $P_t \leq .001$; $R^2 = .983$.

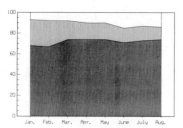

Figure 2.1A. Percent of
Public Support for President
Eisenhower, Jan.-Aug. 1953.

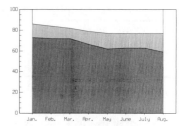

Figure 2.1B. Percent of
Public Support for President
Eisenhower, Jan.-Aug. 1957.

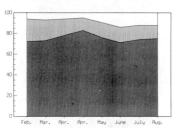

Figure 2.1C. Percent of
Public Support for President
Kennedy, Feb.-Aug. 1961.

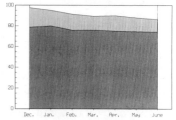

Figure 2.1D. Percent of
Public Support for President
Johnson, Dec. 1963-June 1964.

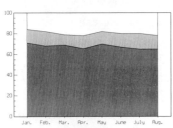

Figure 2.1E. Percent of
Public Support for President
Johnson, Jan.-Aug. 1965.

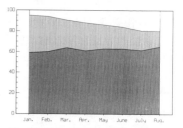

Figure 2.1F. Percent of
Public Support for President
Nixon, Jan.-Aug. 1969.

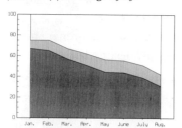

Figure 2.1G. Percent of
Public Support for President
Nixon, Jan.-Aug. 1973.

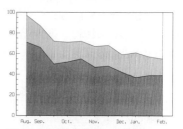

Figure 2.1H. Percent of
Public Support for President
Ford, Aug. 1974-Feb. 1975.

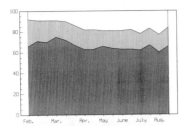

Figure 2.1I. Percent of
Public Support for President
Carter, Feb.-Aug. 1977.

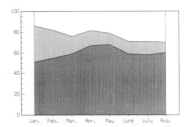

Figure 2.1J. Percent of
Public Support for President
Reagan, Jan.-Aug. 1981.

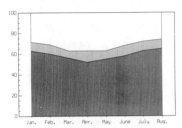

Figure 2.1K. Percent of
Public Support for President
Reagan, Jan.-Aug. 1985.

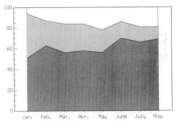

Figure 2.1L. Percent of
Public Support for President
Bush, Jan.-Aug. 1989.

NOTE TO FIGURE 2.1: The unshaded area represents "disapprove," the light cross-hatching "don't know/no opinion," and the intermediate cross-hatching "approve." The poll periods for President Kennedy are correct as indicated. In the Ford and Carter terms there were occasional months with more than one poll.

TABLE 2.1

Trends in Approval in the First Seven Months of a President's Second Term

President	Approval			Relative approval[b]		
	b	t_b	R^2	b	t_b	R^2
Eisenhower	−2.45	−6.07[c]	.86	−2.14	−8.43[c]	.93
Johnson	−0.65	−1.67	.28	−0.51	−1.31	.19
Nixon	−4.92	−9.80[c]	.93	−5.11	−10.45[c]	.94
Reagan	−0.18	−0.21	.01	−0.14	−0.15	.005

Regression statistics[a]

[a] The regression statistics should be interpreted as follows: "b" is the expected monthly change in the measure of approval; "t_b" is a measure of the statistical significance of the "b" coefficient; and "R^2" is a measure (ranging from 0.0 to 1.0) of the estimated fit between the model and the data.
[b] "Relative approval" is the percentage of those with an opinion who approve of the president's job performance; those without an opinion are left out of the denominator.
[c] A "t_b" this large would occur by chance fewer than five times in one hundred.

information processing and opinion formation; it certainly would not reflect a suspension of standard processes.

President Reagan's support level during the early months of 1985 was not at rest either. In this case, a linear model of the early-term period is precisely misleading; the poll figures for the first seven months of President Reagan's second term follow a parabolic path. From January to April 1985, President Reagan's approval rating dropped eleven percentage points— from 63 percent to 52 percent. However, in May a steady recovery began, and by July, at the end of the seven-month period, the eleven percentage points had been restored. This is evidence of a public responding to perceived success and failure, and it is also evidence of the volatility of opinion, but it is not evidence of a "honeymoon" plateau at the beginning of the second Reagan term.

On balance, it would appear that presidents in their second terms do not begin with a special fund of public goodwill. Do they in their first terms? If so, has the "honeymoon" changed in the wake of Vietnam, Watergate, and the Nixon Pardon? Table 2.2 presents a statistical summary of the Gallup Poll data for the first seven months of the eight most recent presidential first terms.

For presidential first terms, there appears to be evidence of a honeymoon period. The proportion of "approvers" in the total sample is relatively steady over the early months. However, "approvers" as a percentage of those with an opinion is far from steady; there are certainly no plateaus in "relative approval." Relative approval declines on the average from about one percentage point per month for President Eisenhower and President Bush to over two and a half percentage points per month for President Nixon. Taken together the patterns displayed by the measures of approval and relative approval argue for the conclusion that over the early months of a new president's term public uncertainty (or reluctance to judge a newly elected president) gives way to declared disapproval.

TABLE 2.2

Trends in Approval in the First Seven Months of a President's First Term

| | Regression statistics[a] | | | | | |
| | Approval | | | Relative approval[b] | | |
President	b	t_b	R^2	b	t_b	R^2
Eisenhower	0.68	1.53	.308	−1.18	−5.82[c]	.856
Kennedy	−0.13	−0.18	.005	−1.49	−3.15[c]	.578
Johnson	−0.77	−3.54[c]	.531	−1.89	−7.89[c]	.846
Nixon	0.28	0.67	.050	−2.75	−7.91[c]	.884
Ford	−5.18	−6.05[c]	.818	−2.32	−4.82[c]	.810
Carter	−1.28	−3.03[c]	.369	−2.32	−4.99[c]	.615
Reagan	0.31	0.65	.396	−1.82	−5.56[c]	.553
Bush	2.15	2.91[c]	.585	−1.11	−1.49	.271

[a]The regression statistics should be interpreted as in Table 2.1: "b" is the expected monthly change in the measure of approval; "t_b" is a measure of the statistical significance of the "b" coefficient; and "R^2" is a measure (ranging from 0.0 to 1.0) of the estimated fit between the model and the data.

[b]"Relative approval" is the percentage of those with an opinion who approve of the president's job performance; those without an opinion are left out of the denominator.

[c]A "t_b" this large would occur by chance fewer than five times in one hundred.

This conclusion is entirely consistent with the model underlying the theoretical sketch with which this chapter began. "Approve" is a socially desirable response and "disapprove" is a socially undesirable response to the Gallup question at the outset of a new administration. Those who, because of partisanship and/or the habit of opposition developed during the campaign, cannot respond positively to the new president in the main cannot respond negatively either. They can safely withhold judgment, and apparently this is what they do. After the early weeks, political elites are given the specifics of the new president's program and some find the courage to pronounce their opposition; then the media take up and retail this commentary. In a word, the social undesirability of a negative response to the Gallup question is reduced by the natural (or at least political) forces operating in a pluralistic political system. The president's opponents in the public respond accordingly; their expression of uncertainty is exchanged for open disapproval.

The group of hardcore opponents that makes evident its predetermined disapproval of the president and/or his program is a minority of the public, but not a tiny minority. Our best guess would be that, depending upon whether the president is a Democrat or a Republican, this group constitutes between one-fifth and one-quarter of the American public.[6] Upwards of two-thirds of the public constitute the early term popularity plateau. Two distinct subgroups combine here. There is a small group of hardcore supporters of the president—the mirror image of his predetermined opponents—who make up the approximately 20 percent who approve of the president's job performance no matter what is revealed about it.

This leaves about half of the total public unaccounted for. This is the group that offers a unanimously positive evaluation of the president early in his term. This unanimity can and usually does break down in light of new information and conflicting elite interpretations of presidential performance, which become available as the honeymoon comes to an end.

It was among this group that President Ford lost support just weeks after he took over from President Nixon. The fact, made clear in Figure 2.1H and Table 2.2, that President Ford rapidly lost public support reveals that a "honeymoon" is not a guaranteed feature of first presidential terms. Upon closer consideration this glaring exception to the general picture actually lends support to the model of public opinion that gives rise to the honeymoon period.

The early months of the Johnson and Carter presidencies show small but regular and statistically reliable declines in public support. These are, however, not worth considering beyond noting that they exist. Both Presidents Johnson and Carter

6. This figure is arrived at by noting that eventually the percentage reporting "no opinion" on presidential job handling comes to rest at about 10 percent. It will fluctuate around this figure due to sampling variation. I have simply subtracted this group from the size of the combined "disapproval" and "no opinion" percentages for the early part of the first presidential terms.

ended the seven-month period with an approval level within one percentage point of the average for the first six months. President Bush's "honeymoon" period is also an exception; this is an artifact of the arbitrary selection of the first seven months for the duration of the "early term" effect. Figure 2.1L indicates that from January through May 1989 President Bush's approval ratings were unexceptional.[7] The events in Eastern Europe ended the honeymoon, but on a very happy note. President Bush's approval ratings, which had plateaued around 55 percent, jumped about 15 percentage points between May and June and thereafter plateaued at nearly 70 percent for the balance of the period under observation.

The Ford period requires further consideration. The three elements that I have hypothesized produce the early term plateaus of presidential support were absent within one month of President Ford's taking office. This can be explained by the fact that he was not elected. This does not mean he was not approved of when he took office. On the contrary, his 71 percent approval rating in his first Gallup Poll, in August 1974, was higher than the first poll figures for Presidents Eisenhower, Nixon, Carter, and Reagan and matched President Kennedy's first poll results. It does appear to mean that his support was less resilient, less resistant to the criticisms of political elites, when they came, than was support for presidents elected to the position or who succeeded from the vice presidency to which they had been elected. In the wake of the political turmoil that led to President Nixon's resignation, the political elite and the media rallied behind President Ford. But his honeymoon with American opinion leaders lasted only a few weeks—only until the presidential pardon and all that that act communicated about the credibility of presidential assurances. It is as if Presi-

7. For the first five months of the term the coefficients—parallel to those found in Table 2.2—for "approval" of President Bush's handling of his job as president were $b = 0.50$, $t_b = 0.322$; $R^2 = .003$; for "relative approval" they were $b = -3.987$; $t_b = -5.835$; $R^2 = .892$.

dent Ford's pardon of President Nixon changed the system that produces public evaluations of presidential performance from the "first term" system to the "second term" system. This proved to be not a fatal disability but the loss of a resource. The pardon may have lost President Ford his honeymoon, but after the initial period the public evaluated President Ford by the same criteria as it did all other presidents (Haight 1978).

The analysis of early term polls can speak directly to the concern that the institution of the presidency itself was transformed for the American people by the crises of confidence emerging from Vietnam, Watergate, and the Nixon pardon. If we use as our criterion of change *transformation of the dynamics of positive evaluation* in the early months of the term, it is hard to support the proposition that a major departure was produced by Vietnam and the crisis of confidence it engendered. Setting aside the Ford Administration, recent presidents are no less likely to enjoy a support plateau early in their term than were the presidents who served before the Vietnam war.

The *dynamics* of public evaluations of presidential performance is not the only route by which we can explore the hypothetical effects of Vietnam, Watergate, and the Nixon pardon on public opinion; we can also consider the effect on the *level* of public support. Granted that support is on a plateau early in a president's term, is that plateau now lower than it used to be?

Figure 2.2 supplies the answer. It indicates the average approval level in the seven presidencies for which adequate data are available. Two factors affect these averages: we find the expected "period" effect and note that a "partisan" effect is also at work. Leaving aside President Ford (whose average is rendered meaningless by the strong trend in the data) and the last two months of President Bush's early term, we find that the level of approval after the Johnson presidency is about ten percentage points below what it was before Vietnam.[8]

8. Just when the change took place cannot be stated with precision, and that of course means that "Vietnam" is used symbolically or even meta-

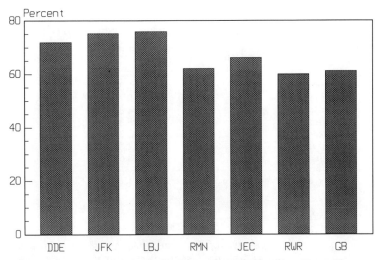

Figure 2.2. Average "Approval" Rating During the First-Term Honeymoon Period.

Within each of these periods, Republican presidents' approval levels are about four percentage points below those of the Democrats, as shown in Tables 2.3 and 2.4. This partisan effect is easily accounted for: over this entire period the number of self-identified Democrats was larger than the number of self-identified Republicans, which translates itself into the relative sizes of the predetermined opposition under Democratic and Republican presidents. Since the early term support plateau is the complement of the size of the predetermined opposition, the imbalance in partisan identification finds expression in support levels as well.

It is more difficult to account for the period effect on the level of honeymoon support. It is easy to say what it cannot be: it cannot be that opposition elites are voicing their opposition

phorically as the precipitating cause of the downgrading of the presidency in public opinion. We can pinpoint the time of change a bit more precisely by noting that the level of approval at the beginning of Johnson's second term was no different than at the beginning of his first term—he averaged 77 percent over the first four months of the second term (before the Dominican Republic crisis rally) and over the first seven months of the first term.

TABLE 2.3

The Partisan Effect on Presidential Approval Levels

President	Mean levels of approval	Variances	No. of polls
Eisenhower	71.9	7.36	8
Kennedy	75.2	10.76	10
Johnson	75.9	4.84	14
Nixon	62.1	5.34	11
Carter	66.1	15.76	16
Reagan	60.0	22.31	13
Bush[a]	56.8	18.66	5

[a]Data for Bush are for the first five months of the term. The Ford presidency is excluded.

TABLE 2.4

Differences in Average Level of Presidential Approval During the First Seven Months: Eisenhower to Bush[a]

	Eisenhower	Kennedy	Johnson	Nixon	Carter	Reagan	Bush
Eisenhower	—	−3.33	−3.98	9.78	5.75	11.90	15.1
Kennedy	−2.18*	—	−0.65	13.11	9.08	15.20	18.4
Johnson	−3.57*	0.56	—	13.76	9.73	15.90	19.1
Nixon	8.00*	−10.14*	−14.76*	—	−4.03	2.10	5.3
Carter	−3.53*	5.87*	7.87*	−2.92*	—	6.10	9.3
Reagan	7.76*	−10.08*	−13.60*	1.62	−4.17*	—	3.2
Bush	7.12*	8.55*	11.91*	2.98*	4.26*	1.24	—

[a]Entries in the upper right triangle of the table are differences between the means of the respective presidents; those in the lower left triangle are t-tests of these differences. A "*" indicates $P_t < .05$.

earlier than they did before Vietnam and that that has lowered the level of the initial fund of public goodwill for the president. Opposition outspokenness may come earlier, but if it registered on public consciousness we would not expect to find a support plateau in the early term of the post-Vietnam presidencies. Under this circumstance, the first Nixon term and the Carter term would look like the Ford term, but they do not.

In a similar vein, the change in the attitudes of the media toward the president brought on by the war in Vietnam (Braestrup 1978) and the change in the value and frequency of investigative journalism wrought by Watergate cannot have directly reduced the level of support. If Vietnam and Watergate had ended the early term "alliance" between the media and the White House (Grossman & Kumar 1981), we would not have a plateau at all. As in President Ford's case, these changes would produce downward trends in support.

To account for the effect of "period" on the level of support during the honeymoon, we need to posit an increase in negative comment by political elite and the media that has not destroyed the alliance phase. This we can do if we recognize that the alliance period is not simply a matter of goodwill—of gifts exchanged, as it were, between the White House and the media—but also a matter of organizational necessity for both parties (Grossman & Kumar 1981: 275–79). Presidents now are presented in a more unfavorable light than they used to be, but against that trend in the growth of unfavorable coverage, the phases in the relationship between the White House and the media are repeated anew for each administration.

The public receives the product of both the trends in negative comment and coverage and the cycle of media-administration relationship and responds accordingly. The cloud of suspicion and cynicism that has enveloped the presidency since Vietnam, Watergate, and the pardon has increased the predetermined opposition to the president. The remaining group—now smaller than it used to be—still works with the information it receives, and since early in the term that information favors the president, the honeymoon plateau continues to appear.

The pre–March 30th polls indicated that President Reagan was likely to have a typical early-term honeymoon. Gallup recorded 51 and 59 percent approval figures for February and March. The relative approval levels for these two polls are 80 and 75 percent. These polls show that President Reagan eliminated neither the period nor the partisan effects on early-term popularity. He was after all a post-Vietnam, Republican president, and his approval level reflected both of these deficits. The attempt on his life made the early part of President Reagan's term untypical for a time. But the rally associated with the assassination attempt dissipated; by mid-June President Reagan's support scores returned to their pre-attack level, and after August the processes that govern the dynamic of opinion formation began to affect the evaluation of his performance as president.

In the end, opinion on President Reagan, indeed, on all the presidents in this study, depends less upon the public's response to him as a person than on the success or failure of his policies to achieve the outcomes he has led the American people to expect. After the honeymoon is over, it is by this standard that the president will be judged.

CHAPTER 3

The Rally Phenomenon in Public Opinion

with Catherine R. Shapiro

THE IRANIAN HOSTAGE CRISIS and the spectacular upwelling of public support for President Carter that accompanied it, the public response to the destruction of Korean Airlines flight 007, the Grenada incident, and more recently the Iceland Summit and the Iran-Contra Affair have rekindled interest in the public's reaction to international crises. Writing in the magazine *Public Opinion*, Karlyn Keene put the response to the Teheran embassy takeover into perspective: "The sudden surge in popularity was massive but it is worth remembering that otherwise it was by no means unique. For years survey researchers have been intrigued by the tendency of Americans to 'rally round the president' in times of international crisis. This phenomenon is apparently unrelated to a president's perceived effectiveness in handling a situation and it also appears to have become more pronounced in the past decade" (Keene 1980: 28).

Keene, in this passage, is reporting a commonplace. It is conventional wisdom that international crises are "special moments" in public opinion. When the nation or its honor is threatened, the public is thought to suspend its usual mode of opinion formation and form ranks behind the president and the flag.[1] External threat gives rise to the belief that one's patriotic duty requires the appearance of solidarity which, in the public at large, manifests itself as an unexpected jump in approval of presidential job performance (Sigelman & Conover 1981 and sources cited by Mueller 1973: 208). In other words, reporters, pollsters, and scholars have hypothesized an upwelling of patriotic support in response to external threats to account for an increase in positive evaluation when by objective criteria the president appears to have failed.

One variant of the "patriotism" explanation emphasizes cohesion: Waltz argues that in "the face of [a crisis event that obsesses the government] the people rally behind their chief executive, as one would expect them to in any cohesive country" (1967: 272). Sigelman and Conover point out that it "is a well-established principle that threats from outside a system promote cohesion within the system. One familiar manifestation of this principle is the tendency of the American people to rally in support of the President when the nation becomes embroiled in international conflicts" (1981: 303).

This explanation leaves two phenomena to be explained: (1) the suspension of processes that would be expected to lead to an erosion of support among those who, on balance, hold a favorable opinion of the president's job performance, and (2) the winning back to the ranks of the president's supporters of a number of those who, on balance, have come to deprecate his handling of the job. Of course, the more erosion is slowed and the greater the winning back, the higher will approval climb. The first phenomenon may be "necessary," but it can never be a "sufficient" condition for a rally. The second phenomenon is

1. Mueller (1973: 208–13) labels the phenomenon "rally-round-the-flag"; most others mention the president specifically. By his phrasing, Mueller indicates that whatever separation may be usual, in a crisis the president and the nation become identified with each other.

a "necessary" condition for a rally, but whether it is "suffi-cient" will depend upon the pre-crisis rate of erosion among supporters. In any event, it is likely that happenings that con-vert disapprovers will sustain supporters in their approval.

International crises and presidential popularity have been examined in the political science literature within the context of two different kinds of studies. First, international crises have been used as independent variables in models that seek to ex-plain the course of presidential popularity over presidential terms in office. Two excellent exemplars of this type of re-search are John E. Mueller's *War, Presidents, and Public Opin-ion* (1973) and Samuel H. Kernell's 1975 dissertation entitled "Presidential Popularity and Electoral Preference: A Model of Short-Term Political Change." Second, shifts of public opinion following an international crisis have been studied in their own right. Examples of this kind of study include J. R. Lee's "Rallying 'Round the Flag" (1977) and Brody and Shapiro's "Pol-icy Failure and Public Support: The Iran-Contra Affair and Pub-lic Assessments of President Reagan" (1989). In the course of this chapter, we review studies of both types. First, however, we begin with the criteria by which potential rally events are identified.

Criteria for Rally Events

What kinds of events are thought to produce the rallying re-sponse and why? John Mueller gives us three criteria for identi-fying events that should rally the public: "In general, a rally point must be associated with an event which (1) is inter-national and (2) involves the United States and particularly the president directly; and it must be (3) specific, dramatic, and sharply focused" (1973: 209). Why "international"? Domestic events, even domestic crises, are said to be politically divisive and, thus, "likely to exacerbate internal divisions" (*ibid.*). Do-mestic crises are expected to produce public conflict within the opinion leadership elite along familiar lines of cleavage. By contrast, the expectation is that during an international crisis either the public automatically rallies behind the flag or, alternatively, those to whom the public looks for opinion leadership are far more apt to support the president or, at least, not to be outspokenly critical of him. Why must it directly involve the United States and especially the president? Other sorts of major international crises are, according to Mueller, "less likely to seem relevant to the average American" or to "engender split loyalties" (*ibid.*). One is tempted to turn this criterion around and define a major international event as one in which the United States is seen or said to be involved. Given the position of the United States in the postwar international system, conflicts between other nations into which the United States does not intrude or upon which the president does not take a position that commits our resources, are, by and large, non-events for the vast majority of the public. They are not front page news, they do not lead off the nightly news, and from the perspective of public opinion on presidential performance they are not happening. Finally and simply, the event must be "specific, dramatic, and sharply focused to assure public attention and interest" (*ibid.*). Kernell adds to this the stipulation that the situation, to be considered an event which can rally the public, must "[make] the front page for at least five consecutive days . . . to guarantee widespread public awareness" (1978: 513).

Brody argues that if a "rally," *per se*, is to be distinguished from the gain in public approval of the president that would be expected to follow any successful policy outcome, then scholarly attention must be focused on those cases in which the outcomes of the crisis events appear to be of questionable success or clear policy failures (Brody & Shapiro 1989).

Mueller (1973: 210) identifies five types of international events that meet his criteria. First are sudden American military interventions in another nation—as for example the Korean invasion (1950), the Lebanon invasion (1958), the Bay of

Pigs (1961), and the Dominican intervention (1965). Second are major military developments in an ongoing war—the Inchon landing in Korea and the Gulf of Tonkin or Tet Offensive in Vietnam. Third are major diplomatic developments—such events as the Cuban missile crisis, the U-2 incident, the announcement of the Truman Doctrine, the Berlin blockade, the Berlin wall, and the Iranian hostage crisis. Fourth are dramatic technological developments—for example, the launching of Sputnik I in 1957 or the first Soviet atomic test. And last are summit meetings between the president and the head of the Soviet Union. The obvious arbitrariness of the distinctions— for example, between summit meetings and other major diplomatic developments—is of no consequence. Mueller does not lead us to expect different responses from the public to different classes of events; rallying is the expected response. In line with this expectation, Mueller finds it analytically convenient to treat presidential honeymoons as rally events (*ibid.*: 211– 12). Kernell chooses to reinstate a distinction between rally events and presidential honeymoons in his coding procedures. He writes, "Certainly something is happening to popularity at the outset of the president's term which needs to be tapped, but to include it as part of the rally variable only prevents us from appreciating the effects of international affairs on popularity" (Kernell 1975: 42).

Mueller notwithstanding, different types of events may lead to the rally response for different reasons, and so his categories may have utility after all. However, the potential utility or lack of utility of these categories should not divert us from focusing on the expectation that Mueller, Kernell (to a lesser extent), and others have about rally events in general. The expectation is that events such as these will command public attention and will engender a noticeably large net positive response to presidential performance. This conventional wisdom is accepted more often by those who use international crises as independent variables in models of long-term presidential popu-

larity than by those who make public response to crisis the
focus of their investigations. In the next section, we examine
both kinds of studies.

Rally Events and Public Opinion: Rallies as Independent Variables

The first studies of rally events and public opinion were those
which used the events as independent variables in models
attempting to trace the "meanderings of the presidential-
popularity trend line for the period since World War II" (Mueller
1973: viii). Mueller's model takes as its dependent variable responses to the Gallup Poll question, "Do you approve or disapprove of the way (the incumbent) is handling his job as president?" The model has four main independent variables: (1) a
"coalition-of-minorities" variable, (2) an "economic slump"
variable, (3) a "war" variable, and (4) a "rally round the flag"
variable. In addition, Mueller includes a dummy variable for
each of the four presidents examined (Truman, Eisenhower,
Kennedy, and Johnson).

Mueller has this to say (*ibid.*: 212) about the construction
of the rally variable:

> The rally-round-the-flag variable is measured by the length of
> time, in years, since the last rally point . . . [and] each rally
> point is given the same weighting in the analysis. One effort
> to soften this rather crude analysis was made. The rally points
> were separated into two groups: "good" rally points (for ex-
> ample, the Cuban missile crisis) in which the lasting effect
> on opinion was likely to be favorable to the president, and
> "bad" ones (for example the U-2 crisis, the Bay of Pigs) in
> which the initial favorable surge could be expected to be rather
> transitory. . . . The differences [between the two groups] were
> small and inconsistent. The public seems to react to "good"
> and "bad" international events in about the same way.

Mueller acknowledges that his rally-round-the-flag variable is not designed to stand on its own within his model, but

rather to account for the upturns in a general downward trend explained primarily by the coalition-of-minorities variable. He finds that the rally variable is statistically significant in the predicted direction and in general "suggests a popularity decline of about 5 or 6 percentage points for every year since the last rally point" (p. 225).

Kernell sets out to refine Mueller's model. He is troubled by Mueller's findings that seem to indicate that the Vietnam War had virtually no independent effect on President Johnson's popularity. The trouble with Mueller's model, according to Kernell (and also with Stimson's model [1976] of a large fickle population segment), is that by using time as an explanatory variable to measure a president's trends in popularity, they are in effect using time to measure time.[2] Hence, the coalition-of-minorities variable and Stimson's enchantment-disillusionment thesis as applied to public opinion can "not *explain* it but rather only *describe* . . . it" (Kernell 1978: 28).

Kernell's independent variables (or "environmental forces") —chronic problems, the economy, and short-term surges—bear a resemblance to Mueller's but are operationalized somewhat differently in line with three general propositions. First, short-term fluctuations in presidential popularity are caused primarily by current events. Second, at any given time the president's popularity reflects his approval level of the preceding month. Third, presidential popularity tends to move toward some equilibrium level. Kernell separates short-term surges into a rally variable and an early term variable for each president. His model indicates that the rescored rally variable is "consistently correlated with approval for all the presidents. The strength of the relationships varies greatly depending on

2. The Stimson thesis will be explored at length in Chapter 4. In essence, Stimson argues that only time matters when it comes to presidential support. In order to win election, presidents promise the public more than they can deliver; with the passage of time the public becomes increasingly aware of the failure of the president to deliver on his promises, and this failure gives rise to a disillusionment that accumulates over the presidential term.

the general overall plateau of popularity upon which they are operating and the political significance of the events themselves" (Kernell 1978: 97).

It should not perplex us overmuch that events such as those that Mueller and Kernell identify as expected rally events will be the raw material of public evaluation of presidential performance—it seems perfectly natural that they should be. But why should the public reaction to these events necessarily be an affirmation of support for presidential performance? There is some evidence suggesting that the popular response is not always favorable (see Brody & Shapiro 1989). In fact, Kernell notes in his discussion of short-term surges that "The negative sign for Johnson suggests that the events occurring during his term may have had a net negative impact on his popularity. Although a final judgment must await an examination of the relationship under the appropriate controls, it may well be that all 'specific, dramatic, and sharply focussed' international developments cannot be assumed to benefit the incumbent president" (Kernell 1975: 42–43).

It is not obviously the case then that, in Nelson Polsby's words, "invariably, the popular response to a president during international crisis is favorable, *regardless of the wisdom of the policies* [the president] *pursues*" (1964: 25, emphasis added). Nonetheless, it is this counterintuitive movement of public opinion—backing the president when his policies have been unwise or even unsuccessful—that has "intrigued" public opinion researchers. It is no trick to explain support when things go well. However, such an explanation also should be able to account for the positive response of the public when things go badly or the outcome is unclear. Rival explanations for both the direction of and the variations in changes in presidential approval levels constitute a second major variety of rally literature.

Rally Events and Public Opinion: Rallies as Dependent Variables

Jong R. Lee begins his article "Rallying 'Round the Flag: Foreign Policy Events and Presidential Popularity" by criticizing what he sees as a major problem with the Mueller model of presidential popularity—namely, the model's assumption that all major international events, or crises, have an identical impact on presidential popularity. As he points out, empirical evidence reveals just the opposite. The purpose of Lee's study is to "examine the impact major international events have on presidential popularity case by case in order to discover patterns of the public's reaction to the President" (1977: 252).

Lee formulates a somewhat looser set of criteria for identifying major international events than the more standard Mueller criteria. For each event that meets the Lee criteria, two measures are taken. First, the magnitude of the rally is measured as the percentage change between responses to the Gallup survey question about whether the respondent approves or disapproves of the way the president is handling his job. Second, the duration of the rally is measured as the number of months it takes before presidential popularity returns to within two percentage points of the pre-event level.

Lee notes that in most cases there is a positive rally following major international events regardless of the success or failure of U.S. policy. Two explanations of this counterintuitive movement of opinion are offered: one emphasizes the effects of the crisis situation on the information available to the public; the other emphasizes the attitudinal response of the public to the challenge inherent in an international crisis. Lee poses the alternatives as follows: "[The] President becomes the focus of national attention in times of crisis . . . symbolizing national unity and power. . . . The average man's reaction will include a feeling of patriotism in supporting presidential action, a desire not to hurt a President's chance of success" (Lee 1977: 253). Alternatively, "[The] public tends to support a presidential action (or inaction at times) regardless of its content, when there is not enough information for evaluating the situation . . . [the] initial reaction of the public to major foreign policy events is to give the president the benefit of doubt" (*ibid.*).

Unfortunately, Lee stops short of testing these two alternatives. He does, however, contribute to the study of rallies in three ways. First, he explores the relationship between a rally's absolute size of popularity change and its duration. He notes correlations between types of international events and duration, and between these event types and absolute change of popularity, but he also notes that no significant correlation between level of popularity change and duration is manifest in his data. Second, Lee disproves the notion that perhaps the magnitude or the duration of rallies depend on who the president is. He writes, "An analysis of variance indicates that the average change of popularity and duration of seven administrations do not differ significantly from one to another. This finding is further confirmed by a regression analysis using a set of dummy variables denoting each Presidency" (*ibid.*: 255). Finally, Lee finds preliminary evidence suggesting a relationship between the salience of an event and the size—although not the duration—of the rally. Salience is measured by the percentage of respondents in Gallup Polls who indicate that they have read or heard about prominent issues. Lee suggests that the salience of an event may influence the size of the popularity change; however, his correlative tests do not give us indication of a causal relationship between the two factors.

Brody and Shapiro (1989) construct a causal model of changes in the levels of approval due to international crises and use it to examine the negative rally associated with the Iran-Contra scandal. Of the two explanations set forth in the Lee article, only the second—that rallies occur in situations in which there is insufficient evaluative information available to the public—can be tested in the model.

In order to determine whether measures of the content of news on the Iran-Contra affair affected public evaluations of President Reagan, total and critical coverage of the Iran-Contra scandal (as measured weekly from the New York *Times* and CBS-TV News) are made a part of analyses designed to account for such evaluations. A two-stage causal model is constructed: at the first stage, the dependent variable is a general evaluation of President Reagan, represented by the 1986 American National Election Study [NES] "feeling thermometer." At the second stage, the dependent variable is the NES replicate of the Gallup Poll and New York *Times*/CBS-TV News Poll item, which queries whether the respondent "approves" or "disapproves" of the "way President Reagan is handling his job as president." The independent variables, in addition to the two weekly news content variables, include gender, partisanship, ideology, political interest, media use, and attitudes toward aid to the Contras. Since general attitude toward President Reagan is measured with a 100 point scale, ordinary least squares regression analysis is used to estimate the first stage of the model; the second stage of the model is estimated with probit analysis. Because of non-random distribution of education levels across the five weeks of the NES study, separate causal models are developed for each of the three educational attainment groups— viz., those with less than a high school education, those whose schooling ended with high school, and those whose schooling went beyond high school.

The results are generally supportive of an opinion leadership explanation of public assessments of presidential performance in times of international crisis, although it must be remembered that only one crisis situation to date has been analyzed in this fashion. For those respondents with less than a high school education, neither total coverage nor amount of critical coverage of the Iran-Contra affair was directly related to their assessments of presidential performance. However, both measures are indirectly related through their impact on the citizens' general opinion of the president. For those respondents who finished high school but did not go beyond it, and for those who have more than a high school education, total volume of news coverage is not related directly or indirectly to opinions about President Reagan. However, the volume of criticism is directly related to assessments of presidential performance.

Rally Data

Getting down to cases, let us consider the movement of public opinion in the wake of 65 events that are potential rally points.[3] The list of events and the change in percent approving of presidential job handling between the last pre-crisis poll and the next Gallup Poll are displayed in Table 3.1. On the whole, opinion change follows the expected course. In 42 of the 65 situations the president picks up support. Twenty-three events were followed by a loss rather than a gain in public support; more than half of these (twelve out of the 23) are clustered in two of Mueller's five categories: six are summit meetings between the president and the leader of the Soviet Union and six are "major military developments in an ongoing war" (1973: 210). The six military developments that do not give rise to a rally are more than half of the situations so classified; the six summits not followed by a rise in public support are two-thirds of the direct meetings between Soviet and American leadership in the postwar period. Looked at another way, of the twenty situations between 1948 and 1986 classified in these two categories, twelve are followed by declines in support for the president and eight are followed by increases in support. One won-

3. The first 41 cases are those found in Kernell's dissertation (Kernell 1975: 48–51), which covers the postwar years through 1972. We have added the nine generally acknowledged rallying events in the last part of the Nixon Administration and in the Ford and Carter Administrations. In addition, we have identified fifteen rallying events in the Reagan Administration through the end of 1986.

TABLE 3.1

Rally Events and the Movement of Public Support for the President

President and event	Percent change in approval
Truman	
Truman Doctrine (Mar. 1947)	+12
Berlin blockade (Apr. 1948)	+ 3
Soviet A-bomb announced (Sept. 1949)	− 6
Korean invasion (June-July 1950)	+ 9
Inchon landing (Sept. 1950)	− 4
China crosses the Yalu River (Nov.-Dec. 1950)	− 3
Korean peace talks begin (July 1951)	+ 4
Eisenhower	
Korean truce signed (July-Aug. 1953)	+ 1
Big Four Geneva conference (July 1955)	+ 4
Sputnik I launched (Oct. 1957)	+ 3
U.S. Marines land in Lebanon (July 1958)	+ 6
Khrushchev visit at Camp David (Sept. 1959)	+ 5
U-2 shot down by Soviets/Paris Summit (May 1960)	+ 3
Kennedy	
Bay of Pigs Incident (Apr. 1961)	+ 5
Vienna Summit (May 1961)	− 3
Berlin Wall (Aug. 1961)	+ 1
Test Ban Treaty (Aug.-Sept. 1961)	+ 4
Berlin Crisis (Oct. 1961)	+ 2
Cuban Missile Crisis (Oct. 1962)	+12
Johnson	
Gulf of Tonkin Incident (Aug. 1964)	− 5
Start of North Vietnam bombing (Feb. 1965)	− 2
Invasion of Dominican Republic (Apr.-May 1965)	+ 6
Extension of North Vietnam bombing (July 1966)	+ 8
Glassboro Summit (June 1967)	+ 8
Pueblo Incident (Jan. 1968)	− 7
Tet Offensive/U.S. Embassy invaded (Jan.-Feb. 1968)	− 7
North Vietnam agrees to peace talks (Apr. 1968)	+ 4
Bombing halt (Nov. 1968)	+ 1
Nixon	
"Vietnamization" speech (Nov. 1969)	+11
Invasion of Cambodia (May 1970)	+ 1
China trip (Feb. 1972)	+ 4
Haiphong harbor mined (May 1972)	− 3
"Peace is at hand" speech (Oct.-Nov. 1972)	+ 6
Christmas bombing (Dec. 1972)	− 8
Vietnam peace agreement (Jan. 1973)	+16
Washington, D.C. Summit (June 1973)	− 5
Arab-Israeli cease fire (May 1974)	+ 3
Moscow Summit (July 1974)	− 2

President and event	Percent change in approval
Ford	
Cambodia falls to Communists (Apr. 1975)	− 5
Mayaguez Incident (June 1975)	+11
Helsinki Summit (July 1975)	− 7
Egypt-Israel Treaty (Aug. 1975)	+ 1
Carter	
Panama Canal Treaty (Aug. 1977)	+ 6
Neutron bomb deferred (Mar.-Apr. 1978)	− 8
Mid-East Summit at Camp David (Sept. 1978)	+ 3
Mid-East Treaty (Mar. 1979)	+ 6
Vienna Summit (June 1979)	− 1
Embassy seized in Teheran (Nov. 1979)	+ 6
Soviet invasion of Afganistan (Dec. 1979)	+ 2
Hostage rescue attempt fails (Apr. 1980)	+ 4
Reagan	
U.S. downs Libyan fighters (Aug. 1981)	− 8
Falklands war (Apr. 1982)	− 2
Bombing at U.S. Embassy in Lebanon (Apr. 1983)	+ 2
South Korean passenger plane shot down by USSR (Sept. 1983)	+ 4
Bombing of Marine compound in Beirut/invasion of Grenada (Oct. 1983)	+ 4
Truck bombing of U.S. Embassy in Beirut (Sept. 1984)	− 3
Kuwait airline hijacking (Dec. 1984)	+ 3
TWA hijacking (June 1985)	+ 3
Palestinians seize cruise ship/U.S. intercepts jet with hijackers (Oct. 1985)	+ 3
Geneva Summit (Nov. 1985)	− 2
U.S. attack on Libya (Feb. 1986)	− 1
U.S. jets attack Libyan targets (Mar. 1986)	− 1
Daniloff detention in USSR/Pan Am jet hijacking (Aug.-Sept. 1986)	+ 1
Nicaragua shoots down U.S. plane/captures Hasenfus (Oct. 1986) & Reykjavik Summit (Oct. 1986)	+ 4
Iran-Contra Affair (Nov. 1986)	−21

ders whether categories that do no better than a coin flip should not be dropped from the set of putative occasions for the rallying of public opinion.

If the rally phenomenon is a way of accounting for *otherwise inexplicable* rises in support for the president in the face of surprise and threat, ongoing wars and summit meetings would seem unlikely occasions for rallies. Summits seldom surprise, and even less frequently are they crises in the sense that they threaten national well-being. Summits usually are occasions for pomp and ceremony and result in the ratification of agreements previously arranged between foreign policy nego- tiators for the two nations—though the Paris Summit break- down following the U-2 incident and the Reykjavik Summit were quite different from other summits in these respects. Ongoing wars would seem an unlikely place to look for rally events in any case. They are "international" and do "directly involve" the U.S. and the president, to be sure, but they are, because of sustained media attention, political situations about which the public and the opinion leaders are unusually well in- formed. Both summits and military developments are, in other words, situations that do not call for giving the president the "benefit of doubt" (Lee 1977: 253). Nor can it be said that "there is no time for dissension to develop" (Waltz 1967: 273). They are situations in which the bases of judgment of presidential performance are available, and the public appears to respond accordingly.

Figure 3.1 illustrates the effect of including or excluding

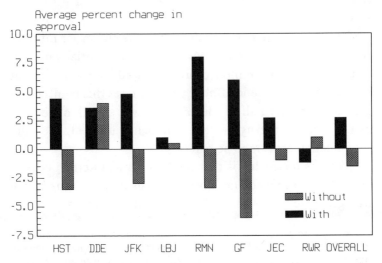

Figure 3.1. Rally Events and Change in Support With and Without Summit Meetings and "Major Military Events."

the twenty cases of Soviet-U.S. summit meetings and "major military developments" on our appreciation of the rally phenomenon. This figure indicates the average percentage point difference in approval in the polls that bracket the onset of a putative rally point. Solid bars are averages for all types of "rally events" except summit meetings and "major military developments"; the cross-hatched bars are the averages for these two types of events. Although they vary considerably from one presidency to another, the average change in presidential support for three of Mueller's categories—"sudden American intervention," "major diplomatic developments," and "dramatic technological developments"—is positive for all of the postwar presidents except President Reagan. The changes in support associated with summits and "major military developments" is positive in only three of the eight presidencies. The overall mean change in support is positive (mean = 2.71, s^2 = 37.98, n = 45) for the non-summit, non-military events, and negative (mean = -1.55, s^2 = 21.42, n = 20) for the summits and military events. The difference between these means is substantial and statistically significant (Δ = 4.26, t = 2.72, df = 63, $p_t \leq$ .005).

The 45 cases remaining, after summits and major military developments have been removed, show substantial variation in the amount of opinion change evinced by the polls that bracket their occurrence. Table 3.2 illustrates this point. However, since nearly half of the cases show a growth of support that is outside the 95 percent confidence interval, the rally phenomenon appears to be real.[4]

What is unsettling is that the Mueller and Kernell criteria for choosing events do not give us a basis for predicting which will give rise to the rally effect and which will not. A com-

4. For base percentages in the range where approval normally falls (20–80 percent), on a random basis we would expect 5 percent of new samples to differ by more than 3 percentage points. With 45 cases, 5 percent would be 2.25 cases; we find 21.

TABLE 3.2

Opinion Change in Forty-Five Rally Situations
(Based on ungrouped data)

	Range of percentage point change in approval							
	−21 to −9	−8 to −5	−4 to 0	1 to 3	4 to 6	7 to 9	10 to 12	13 plus
Number	1	4	4	15	15	1	4	1
Percentage	2.2	8.9	8.9	33.3	33.3	2.2	8.9	2.2

NOTE: Mean = 2.7, s^2 = 37.98, n = 45.

parison of a few event-cases that are more than superficially similar illustrates this point.

The *Mayaguez* incident (May 12, 1975) is one of the prime examples of a rally point. The trigger of the incident was the Cambodian Navy's seizing of the merchant ship *Mayaguez* in the Gulf of Thailand. In the Gallup polls that bracket the incident President Ford's approval rating moved up eleven percentage points (from 40 to 51 percent) despite the fact that in the successful rescue of the 39 members of the *Mayaguez* crew, 38 U.S. Marines and airmen were killed and 50 more were wounded. In addition to the U.S. casualties, the international political fallout from the application of military force in the region raised questions about the wisdom of the action—for example, Thailand protested, and American personnel in Laos had to be evacuated—but the public formed up behind the president and gave him a boost in popularity that postponed the erosion of his support for about three months.

The *Pueblo* incident (January 23, 1968) bears a family resemblance to the *Mayaguez* incident and yet, as far as we can tell, the public completely failed to rally behind President Johnson. Like the *Mayaguez*, the *Pueblo* was a U.S. ship captured by an Asian Communist nation in international waters. In the case of the *Pueblo*, no rescue mission was attempted and no lives were lost. The North Koreans put on a show trial and produced a "confession" by the captain of the *Pueblo*, and eventually this incident ended with the release and repatriation of the crew. In the Gallup polls that bracket the onset of the incident President Johnson's approval ratings dropped from 48 percent to 41 percent.

Before we hazard an explanation let us satisfy ourselves that the failure of the *Pueblo* to rally the American public is not an isolated happening. The downing of the U-2 spy plane by the Soviet Union in May 1960 is associated with a three percentage point gain in approval for President Eisenhower, but nine years later when North Korea shot down our EC-121 electronic surveillance plane, President Nixon's approval rating got no boost (it stood at 63 percent in late March before the incident and at 62 percent in the first poll that followed it in May 1969). The U.S. Marine landings in Lebanon in 1958 and in Santo Domingo in 1969 are associated with six percentage point gains in President Eisenhower's and President Johnson's popularity, but when the Marines went into Cambodia in May 1970 President Nixon's approval rating gained a statistically trivial one percentage point. The Berlin blockade is associated with a three percentage point rise in President Truman's job rating, but the two Berlin crises in 1961 benefited President Kennedy hardly at all—one percentage point when the Wall went up in August and two points when the Berlin crisis blossomed in October. Finally, in the wake of the Viet Cong invasion of our embassy in Saigon at the start of the Tet Offensive in 1968, President Johnson dropped seven percentage points; President Carter, on the other hand, gained six points in the first poll after our embassy in Teheran was taken over.[5]

The variation in response to apparently similar international events is clear. It rules out any simple explanation of the rally phenomenon when it occurs. However, it seems unlikely that the public rallies behind the president because of a reflexive patriotic response. Why should the *Mayaguez* call forth pa-

5. It should be noted that the capture of the *Pueblo* and the invasion of the U.S. embassy in Saigon happened in the same poll period. Their effects on public support are not separable.

triotism and the *Pueblo* not? Why Lebanon and Santo Domingo and not Cambodia? In the abstract, why is the invasion
of the embassy compound in Saigon less an occasion for threat
to induce a cohesion driven by patriotism than the invasion of
the embassy compound in Teheran a decade later? In the "rally
'round the flag" thesis, there is no reason for the variation in
response. One alternative is, of course, that the response is
contingent or context-dependent, but the very idea of a context-
dependent reflex is peculiar indeed. If we require contextual
elements to help us account for the public's response to international crises, why posit a reflexive response at all? Parsimony
would urge us to go as far as we can with the elements of context alone before bringing a special psychological response into
the account.

Opinion Leadership and the Rally Response

If we do not assume that international crises are "special moments" that call forth a peculiar (or at least particular) public
response, how can we account for the rally phenomenon when
it does happen? If we posit the principle that the public works
with available information and hypothesize that international
crises can substantially alter the normal partisan character of
the political information the public is offered, we can develop a
straightforward account of the rally phenomenon.

The account begins with Waltz's assertion that in crisis
"there is no time for dissension to develop" (1967: 273). However cryptic, this assertion contains a compelling political insight: when events are breaking at an unusually rapid pace,
when the administration has a virtual monopoly of information about the situation, opposition political leaders tend to re-
frain from comment or to make cautiously supportive statements. Opposition spokespersons are motivated to alter their
normal stance by an unknown (probably unknowable) mix of
patriotism and outrage at the threat to the country and the

desire not to appear stupid and intemperate as the situation becomes clearer. Opposition elites, in other words, have substantial incentive to remain silent or to be vaguely supportive—support that later can be, and usually is, withdrawn—and almost no incentive to criticize the president. The only opinion leaders with a substantial incentive for negative comment are those with a constituency sufficiently radical to expect such comments from its leaders no matter what. For most purposes and in most circumstances, opposition leaders with this kind of radical constituency are not legitimate sources of opinion leadership for the public nor legitimate news sources for the media.

When crises alter the incentives for most opinion leaders to speak out on the issues, they likewise will affect the normal mix of evaluative comment available to the public through the media. When legitimate sources of opposition comment are silent or supportive of presidential action, reporters and editors will either have to carry an unusually uncritical mix of news about presidential performance or risk the appearance of searching out negative comment for its own sake. Under these circumstances, finding a "balance" to news originating from the White House or from administration-controlled sources in the field, in the midst of a fast-breaking international crisis, would require the media to violate its own professional norms and practices. Seeking negative comment from non-legitimate sources, when legitimate sources are positive or silent, is both unprofessional and unnecessary. The intrinsic drama of an international crisis is sufficient in itself and relieves reporters and editors of the usual need to dramatize stories by reporting political conflict or the policy debate between opposing elites. In crises reporters and editors can satisfy their need for interesting news without risking the damaging appearance of being out to "get" the president.

At this point, it is useful to make clear what we mean when we refer to "elites" or "opinion leaders." For "elite" we could have easily substituted "source," in the sense that the term is used by reporters and editors. We refer to individuals—often but not exclusively government officials—who by role, experience, or expertise are in a position to comment on matters of public concern and are seen to be in that position by those who would contribute to public understanding of these matters. It is a status that is conferred by election, by appointment, and by selection by the news media. A few such individuals—the president, the vice president, candidates for the presidency, the majority and minority leadership of the House and Senate, and a few present and former key staff members in the White House—have this status across the full range of issues of public policy. Most other members of the elite—such as committee and subcommittee chairs and other ranking committee members—have much more circumscribed expertise and consequently are treated as news sources only in policy areas that match this expertise.

Thus, on matters of foreign policy, we would expect the news media to seek comments from committee and subcommittee chairs, from ranking members, and from members of Congress who are otherwise prominent on the House Foreign Affairs and Senate Foreign Relations committees and on the Armed Services and Intelligence committees of the House and Senate.[6] Of course, key individuals in the departments of State and Defense will also be treated as sources; so too will a very limited number of members of the "shadow government"—for example, at the Brookings Institution or the Arms Control Association, in the present administration. On some issues of foreign policy, academic experts will also be called upon for comment.

This account is not meant to deny that these political leaders, reporters, editors, and even members of the public at large may be more patriotic when the nation is threatened; we have

6. Key members of the staff of these committees will also be treated as sources but seldom identified by name—either because of their own reluctance or because the reporter or editor believes that the name will contribute less credibility than the mention of the staff role.

no evidence on the question one way or the other, but we have no doubt that some (perhaps many) rally to the flag at such times. Our account argues that we may be able to explain the rally phenomenon, when it occurs, without resort to the patriotism hypothesis, by tracing coverage of the crisis in the media with certain expectations informing our investigations. If these expectations are met, they will yield the twin advantages of (1) preparing us for the difference in coverage in situations that appear to be rally events to which the public does not respond as expected, and (2) relieving us of the need to construct an explanation of why one situation causes an upwelling of patriotism when another, apparently similar situation does not.

What expectations flow from the account based upon hypothesized shifts in elite incentives under uncertainty, and what is the effect of those shifts upon evaluative comment available to the public? Quite simply, press and television accounts of the "politics" surrounding the event will be unusually full of bipartisan support for the president's actions. Political figures from whom we would normally expect negative comment on presidential performance will instead be silent or supportive. In other words, if we develop a list of people to whom the media would normally turn for the comments that provide dramatic political perspective on presidential action, we would find fewer than usual commenting and even fewer commenting negatively.

Such individuals provide opinion leadership for the public. When they rally to the president or run for cover, the public will be given the implied or explicit message "appearances to the contrary notwithstanding, the president is doing his job well." Given this message, it is not surprising that, in the aggregate, the public rallies behind the president. When opinion leadership does not rally or run for cover, the media must and do report this fact. The public now receives countervailing elite evaluations of presidential performance and, in the aggregate, appears to look to the events themselves for information with which to update its judgment of how well the president is handling his job.

Some Case Examples

A brief examination of a pair of cases shows these processes at work. The *Mayaguez* incident broke into the news on May 12, 1975, and ceased to be a leading news story ten days later; at no time during this period did any negative comment by a recognized opposition leader make front-page news. This means, of course, that during the *Mayaguez* incident, President Ford and Secretary Kissinger were the principal sources for news upon which the public could base its evaluation. By contrast, in the crisis provoked by the seizing of the *Pueblo*, President Johnson's policy came under attack by Republican senators four days after the story broke. The public rallied behind President Ford but not behind President Johnson.

The U-2 incident provides more informal evidence on the behavior of opinion leadership in these situations. The story broke into the news on May 6, 1960 (just as the campaigns for the presidential nominations were getting under way). The Washington *Post* that morning carried reports of verbal attacks on the Soviet Union and Khrushchev by members of Congress but no reports of any criticism of President Eisenhower or Secretary Herter. Two days later, after the president admitted the plane had been spying but claimed it was a necessary action, the *Post* carried a page two report of a broadside attack by the Americans for Democratic Action on President Eisenhower's policies, but the attack included no mention of the U-2 incident. Again, the next day (May 9), the *Post* carried a page one story by Warren Unna that included the judgment "official Washington is still grasping for what it should think about the sensational incident." It was not until May 17, 1960, after the Soviet Union walked out of the Paris Summit meeting, that any negative comment by an opposition leader made the papers. That day the front page of the Washington *Post* carried a story on bipartisan congressional support for the president and a bipartisan attack on Khrushchev, but on page seven a story appeared reporting Adlai Stevenson's characterization of the U-2 flight as a "blunder." The Stevenson criticism was undercut, for those Americans who were aware of it—page seven of the *Post* does not routinely reach all newspaper readers—by further front-page stories of bipartisan support on May 18th and 20th. The first real cracks in this united front appeared on May 21st, and the *Post* reported on May 23rd that the collapse of the Paris Summit and, by implication, the U-2 incident were to be Democratic campaign issues in the 1960 presidential election. The crisis had finally become politicized eighteen days after it began.

President Eisenhower did not get a very large boost in approval in the wake of the U-2 incident—his support rose but three percentage points in the polls that bracketed the incident. Even this minor effect appears to have cycled with press reports of dissent within the political elite. The rally boost followed a parabolic course that reached its maximum about eight days into the crisis. The upwelling of support was still at its peak when bipartisan support broke down after eighteen days. Forty days after the U-2 incident first broke into the news its rally effect had totally dissipated.

Following the "Bay of Pigs incident" there was a rally behind President Kennedy—his approval rating rose five percentage points. But was the American political elite uncritical of his actions? The story broke in the New York *Times* on April 17, 1961, with reports that Cuba had been invaded by exiled patriots. At the United Nations, Cuba publicly accused the United States of both planning the intervention and bombing three Cuban airfields. Although three column inches were devoted to reports of demonstrations by pro-Castro sympathizers, there was no reported criticism by American elites on that day. On April 18th, we find two instances of elite criticism of the president, but both had to do with President Kennedy's actions before the Bay of Pigs incident began and both were buried at the back of the first news section. On page eighteen, there were thirteen lines (less than two column inches) of criticism from Senate Foreign Relations Committee member Homer Capehart, who took Kennedy to task for having stated on April 12th that the United States would not intervene in Cuba with armed forces. Editorialist Arthur Krock also criticized the president for having made such a commitment. There was no elite criticism in the *Times* on April 19th (although there were reports of pro-Castro picketers outside the United Nations), and when it was announced on April 20th that two American citizens had been executed by the Cuban government, even Republicans expressed support for President Kennedy.

By April 21st, New York *Times* coverage began to focus on the damage caused by the Bay of Pigs incident to the United States. The bulk of such coverage consisted of bad news rather than criticism of President Kennedy's actions; however, there was a brief mention on page four that Secretary of State Dean Rusk, Under-Secretary Chester Bowles, and various unnamed officials both inside and outside the CIA had been against the plan to aid the Cuban rebels and that Senator Fulbright, Chair of the Senate Foreign Relations Committee, had written privately to President Kennedy expressing his opposition to the plan. The *Times* noted that, in spite of the large amounts of criticism leveled at the United States by other countries, American politicians were refraining from making critical remarks about the president's actions. A reporter wrote, "Republicans may find it hard to resist the temptation to exploit a miscalculation by the Kennedy Administration. They may be inhibited, however, by President Eisenhower's involvement in the beachhead project and his inaction while . . . Dr. Castro was gaining power" (p. 4). In fact, several notable Republicans publicly pledged full support to Kennedy in the following week, including former President Eisenhower, Richard Nixon, Senator Barry Goldwater, and Governor Nelson Rockefeller.

By April 23rd there was speculation that the congressional

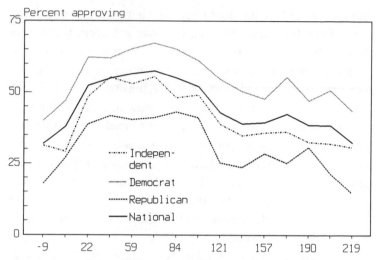

Figure 3.2. Public Support for President Carter During the Iran Hostage Crisis.

"moratorium" on criticism of the president's actions was coming to an end. Criticism of the CIA had already begun to appear in the media. On the 25th, Democratic Senator Wayne Morse was quoted on the front page of the New York *Times* as calling the whole Bay of Pigs incident a "colossal mistake." There was more speculation that, as the situation moderated, Republicans were going to be increasingly vocal in their criticism of President Kennedy. But it was not until April 28th that Republican elites began to make critical comments in their speeches and press releases.

The rally of public support in the wake of the seizing of hostages in our embassy in Teheran was both more intense and longer-lived than the rallies following the U-2 and Bay of Pigs incidents, but we can see similar forces at work on public opinion. In the first place, as Figure 3.2 shows, the public response was wholly "nonpartisan," with members of both major parties and independents reacting in similar ways to President Carter's performance during the first five months of the crisis. The curves mapping performance approval for the party groups are not only remarkably similar but reach their respective maxima within a day or two of one another.[7] They differ in the expected party differences in maxima but in no other particular; indeed, this fact justifies labeling the hostage crisis as a "rally" event. If a rally is anything, it must reflect nonpartisan public responses.[8] Second, the public responded as if to a single source or to multiple harmonizing sources. If there were discordant voices available, the public acted as if they did not exist.

The nonpartisan response of the public has already been documented, but was the information available to the public sufficiently "harmonious" to eliminate the need for hypothesizing an upwelling of patriotism? Recall that in the *Pueblo* incident President Johnson enjoyed only a few days' respite before sustained opposition criticism emerged and was reported. In the U-2 incident President Eisenhower was free from criticism for a fortnight. When we compare these with President Carter's freedom from sustained criticism for at least six weeks, we can begin to understand why the president's job approval rating prospered in the manner depicted in Figure 3.2.

At the time the hostage crisis began, President Carter was a long way from being free of criticism, actual or potential. Two important rivals for the Democratic nomination were about to launch their campaigns and a whole field of Republican nominees were going public with the message that they were the

7. The three regressions yield the following curves:

Party/Group	Maximum(M)	β	Focus(F)	R^2
Democrats	61.8%	−.0013	93.0 days	.57
Independents	48.0%	−.0013	84.8 days	.53
Republicans	38.3%	−.0013	85.4 days	.59

The expected approval level on any given day (D) is found from the equation $E(v) = M + b(F - D)^2$.

8. Sigelman & Conover, with individual-level data, find that there is no significant effect of partisanship in their December 1979 and February 1980 surveys. Only as the "crisis wears on for a few months does partisanship become linked with support for the President" (1981: 312). The aggregate data indicate that the rally effect was fully dissipated by April 1980 and that partisan and other effects on approval reemerged to affect performance evaluations.

best choice to correct the "mess" that the Carter Administration had made of American public policy. Given so large a group of respected political leaders who were routinely providing negative evaluations of presidential performance, it is striking that Iran was not immediately seized upon as yet another instance of President Carter's inadequacy.

The dozen or so aspirants to the presidency who had regularly been criticizing President Carter's domestic and foreign policy would not, could not, or in any case did not try to score off of the foreign policy problems made manifest by the seizure of the embassy. There were exceptions: John Connally, on November 5, 1979, one day after the seizure of the hostages, opined that "if appeasement were an artform, this administration would be the Rembrandt of our time." This one-liner got exactly two lines on page fourteen of that day's Washington *Post*, but was not reported in the New York *Times*. It was mentioned on the CBS Evening News but not on ABC or NBC. Governor Connally tried out the criticism a couple of more times in November and apparently came to the conclusion it was unhelpful. He reversed himself on December 1, 1979, offering the judgment that "we have only one president. Now is the time to rally behind him and show a solid front to Iran and the world." Alexander Haig two weeks into the crisis made the Washington *Post* but none of the networks with his opinion that President Carter's ruling out the use of military force to free the hostages was "the worst thing we can do in one of these situations." Neither Haig's nor Connally's early remarks sparked routine criticism from the remaining group of Republican contenders for the nomination. The opposition fell silent.

On the Democratic side the only notable comment came from Senator Kennedy. On December 2nd, four weeks into the crisis and three weeks into his announced race for the nomination, Senator Kennedy went public with his feelings about the Shah and his regime. Although the President was not mentioned specifically, Kennedy's comments were widely interpreted as critical of Carter and damaging to the president's efforts to save the hostages. (Note the front-page *Post* article by T. R. Reid and D. Broder of Dec. 2, 1979.) Overwhelmingly negative editorial and op-ed responses to Kennedy's comments probably encouraged the opinion leadership in its apparent belief that criticizing the president was not a useful activity.

With legitimate opinion leadership by and large positive or at least not openly critical about President Carter's handling of the situation in Iran, the events themselves and the interpretation put on them by the administration became the principal basis for founding a judgment of Carter's job performance during the first 60 days of the crisis. Beyond 60 days the pace of criticism quickened, and public opinion gradually began to turn around about two weeks later.

More recent international crises further illuminate these processes. President Reagan's job approval ratings were sharply higher following the destruction of KAL-007, but the rally stalled with the rising chorus of criticism from his conservative confreres. Figure 3.3 displays a comparison of trends in media coverage and trends in presidential job approval during this pe-

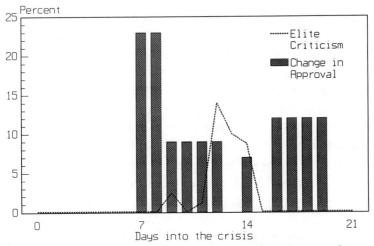

Figure 3.3. Elite Criticism in the Press (Measured as a Percent of New York *Times* Lineage) and Public Opinion on President Reagan During the KAL-007 Crisis (Change in Approval Indexed Against an Aug. 1983 Baseline of 43 Percent).

riod. The two move in tandem. When the media presented criticism of the president's actions—in this instance, inaction—the rally leveled off; when the critics fell silent, the president regained some of his rally-generated approval increase.

The same dynamic appeared during the period in which the bombing of the Marine barracks in Beirut and the invasion of Grenada took place. The two events are intertwined in time and in the attention they received. Public opinion appears to have responded to elite commentary about Grenada, because opposition alignments over the Caribbean crisis were simpler and clearer than they were in the Lebanon crisis.

President Reagan's Gallup approval rating stood at 48 percent when our troops landed on Grenada on October 26, 1983, and that level persisted while House Speaker O'Neill and most of the Democratic congressional delegation voiced opposition to the invasion. On October 27th, President Reagan spoke to the American people. The polls taken in the wake of the speech show no gain in the president's overall job approval rating but evidence the usual public support for the foreign policy actions of the president. Majorities of the public approved of the sending of troops to Grenada and expressed confidence in President Reagan's handling of the crisis. After October 27th, the Democrats began to mute their criticism of the invasion of Grenada. Whether the Democrats' response stemmed from the president's speech, from public approval of the action *per se*, or from the success of the operation cannot be determined. But regardless of its causes, the retreat of the Democrats registered with the public; the Gallup Poll covering the first two weeks of November 1983 shows a five percentage point gain in President Reagan's approval level. In these cases, too, the public appears to respond to opinion leadership.

In October 1986, President Reagan and Soviet General Secretary Gorbachev met at the Reykjavik Summit (or "presummit") to discuss the future of arms control and disarmament talks. Polls bracketing the summit meeting show a four percent increase in aggregate public approval of the way the president handled his job. A review of the news coverage for the period of the summit shows that elite commentary critical of the president's policy proposals was virtually absent. This absence is not for want of attention to the summit: from October 13 to October 19, 1986, the New York *Times* devoted nearly one-fifth (18.6 percent) of its front-page lineage to the summit and its aftermath. CBS News gave the same signal by devoting more than a fifth (21.5 percent) of its total broadcast time to the summit and its aftermath.[9] In neither medium, however, was much space devoted to elite criticism of presidential policy at the summit or on arms control. The *Times* used about one-quarter of one percent of its front-page lineage to report elite criticism. CBS devoted less than one percent of its broadcast time (.85 percent) to critical elite commentary on the summit (Brody & Shapiro 1989).

In contrast to media coverage of the Reykjavik Summit, coverage of the Iran-Contra affair during November 1986 was full of elite criticism directed both at the president and at his policy initiative. Interestingly, a significant portion of the criticism came from Republican members of Congress and from administration officials—such as Secretary of State George Shultz —who normally would be expected to support the president's position at such a time. On CBS News, elite criticism accounted for more than 24 percent of the news time devoted to the Iran-Contra affair in its first four weeks. In the New York *Times* over 20 percent of the Iran-Contra affair coverage was critical of President Reagan. These extraordinarily high levels of critical commentary are all the more surprising given that even before

9. With television news it is easy to determine the total news hole—it averages 22 minutes per day and deviates only slightly from that average. For the New York *Times* comparisons of the total news hole over time are less meaningful. The total news hole expands and contracts with the weekly advertising cycle and has less to do with news, *per se*, than does time devoted to a given topic on television. However, front-page lineage is fixed, so we can use that fact to make meaningful comparisons of attention to a given topic.

the Meese disclosure (which linked the Iranian arms shipments to funding of the Contras) Democratic leaders such as Edward Kennedy were urging party members to tone down such comments in order to avoid appearing too prosecutorial.[10]

Op-Ed Opinion Leadership

There is an interesting and puzzling sidelight to the behavior of opinion leadership during the hostage crisis and the other cases we have examined. One group of opinion leaders routinely fails to run for cover or "rally" to the president: the columnists whose opinions are found on the op-ed pages of the New York *Times* and the Washington *Post* and, through syndication, reach deeply into America. At least one major columnist repeatedly has taken strong exception to presidential policy-making during these international situations. During the U-2 incident Walter Lippmann questioned the wisdom of Eisenhower's policies. Anthony Lewis labeled the military reaction to the seizing of the *Mayaguez* as a serious "over-reaction." Lewis had three critical columns on *Mayaguez*, and in the final one (May 26, 1975) he attacked Senator Church for supporting President Ford's action "from start to finish." No less vehement were Joseph Kraft's and Robert Novak's columns repeatedly criticizing Carter's handling of the hostage crisis.

The puzzle is not over why these columnists failed to rally behind the president. Yea-saying is not part of their job description, although nay-saying may be. Rather the puzzle arises over their apparent lack of influence. Columnists are regarded as opinion leaders and are influential with other opinion leaders and with the public (Grossman & Kumar 1981: 212; Page, Shapiro & Dempsey 1986: 18). The solution to the puzzle is not at hand. Perhaps their reputation for influence is ill-founded, or perhaps their lead in these situations is simply insufficient to

10. For a full-blown analysis of the impact of the Iran-Contra incident on public opinion, see Brody and Shapiro 1989.

encourage opposition political leaders to give voice to criticism (which is to say, of course, that they can lead other opinion leaders only when other values do not intervene). Perhaps the solution lies no deeper than the fact that editorial and op-ed pages often (but not invariably) carry columns with judgments contrary to those we have cited—Joseph Alsop called our aerial spying on the Soviet Union "wonderful news," and James Reston labeled *Mayaguez* "a famous victory." However, although President Carter did pretty well on the editorial page, it is hard to find much support for him among the columns in November and December 1979. That there is no easy solution to the puzzle of the conditional nature of the influence of the columnists—if they are influential at all—does not mean there is no solution. It does mean that our purpose in this chapter is not served by devoting to this puzzle the kind of attention it deserves.

Summary

This chapter has attempted to make several points. First, the rally phenomenon is far from automatic, let alone autonomic. One can easily identify international crises that meet Mueller's criteria in which no significant positive rally took place. And yet rallies occur with sufficient frequency to make it unlikely that we are fooling ourselves into trying to explain random movements of public opinion. Second, the fact of different responses to similar international crises makes it unsatisfying to hypothesize that the rally is caused by an upwelling of patriotism in the face of some international threat. Third, one alternative explanation is that the public responds to opinion leadership. Opposition leaders in some crisis situations lose their incentive to criticize presidential performance, and when this happens, the public rallies. In aggregate terms, a lack of critical opinion leadership can outweigh even relatively unambiguous evidence of policy failure and hence pave the way for positive evaluations of presidential performance. A corollary of this hypothesis is that when opinion leadership is both divided and vocal, such that it offers contradictory evaluations of presidential performance, the public's response will be tied in greater measure to the indications of policy success or failure evinced by the events themselves.

We will examine this explanation in detail in the next section of the book, specifically in Chapter 6. But before detailing that argument, we will consider other accounts of the dynamics of public support for the president.

Presidential Popularity
After the Honeymoon

Presidential Popularity After the Honeymoon

WHAT DETERMINES THE public's evaluation of presidential performance after the honeymoon is over and in the absence of "rally" events? The question is far from settled, but families of explanations can be identified that are distinguished by the degree of control they imply the president has over the factors affecting his standing. Similarly, these explanations also differ in their implications for the linkages between presidential popularity and public policy.

The next five chapters take up explanations that range in implied level of presidential control from none (explanations emphasizing "time" as the key element—a factor over which the president has presumably no control) to considerable (those emphasizing the president's skill as a policymaker). Chapter 4 will consider "time" and presidential popularity. Chapter 5 will explore the relationships between the performance of the macroeconomy and evaluations of presidential job performance. Chapter 6 will examine the relationship between news reports of policy successes and failures and the dynamics of public evaluation of the president. Chapter 7, building on the model developed in Chapter 6, will focus on the presidencies of Kennedy, Johnson, Nixon, and Ford. Chapter 8 will expand the set of cases and increase the complexity of the model by examining the Carter and Reagan presidencies in detail. After these five chapters, we will consider the implications of our findings in Chapter 9.

CHAPTER 4

Of Time and Presidential Popularity

TIME IS POWERFULLY RELATED TO a president's standing with the public. Only three of the thirteen presidential terms since 1945 (the two Eisenhower terms and President Reagan's first term) have failed to show a clear trend of loss of support for the incumbent, who has ended with fewer Americans than he began with approving of his job handling. This trend is evident but is not self-explanatory. The meaning of "time" as an explanatory factor is illusive: if we do not understand why a president loses support with each passing month, then time *per se* cannot offer much insight into the linkage between public policy and public opinion.

Those who use time to explain popularity have offered rationales in terms of political process. Consider Stimson's explanation (1976: 10) of the trend in support: "The president . . . is largely a passive observer of his downsliding popularity. Its causes lie more in the misperceptions of the electorate than in a president's actions. It would therefore occur no matter what he did." In other words, in each successive period of "time," more and more of those who initially supported the president change their minds. This happens not because of any action on his part but because of a defect in how the public forms its opinions. In Stimson's account the public suffers from both "unrealistic" expectations about the results a president can achieve and a lack of interest in the details of the work he has to do in order to attain even limited results. These twin defects "ensure the inevitability of later disillusionment. Because the public, and particularly its ill-informed segments, expects more than can possibly be achieved under the best of circumstances, it is always prone to great disappointment over what is actually achieved by merely mortal presidents acting under less than ideal conditions. Early naive expectations lead to later cynicism" (*ibid*.: 9–10).

Stimson holds the president himself partly responsible for the public's overblown expectations through the presidential campaign, which is directly implicated in creating these expectations. Curiously, he does not hold the president accountable for succeeding or failing in achieving the results he has led the public to expect—he declares the public "naive" for expecting results at all. Stimson and the "better-informed" (according to his account) are satisfied if the president merely pursues his promised policies.

This is a perverse and unnecessarily cynical view of public opinion formation. If it is accurate, it frees a president of any policy constraint stemming from public opinion. If mass opinion is unrelated to presidential action, the president is free to choose any policy option he can sell to the other branches of government. Succeed or fail, his policies will not enter into the public's opinion of him. Under this view there is no public constraint except that which forms in response to the actions of other political elites, who in turn act to constrain presidential policy. This seems an unpromising avenue along which to search for the link between public opinion and public policy. The public is much less likely to know about the actions of other branches of the political system—if for no reason other than that the president's words and deeds are more likely than those of any other political actor to reach the public through the news media (Gans 1979: 9).

At root, Stimson's theory is unsatisfactory because it assumes a quality of information-processing on the part of the public that seem hard to square with what we otherwise know and with Stimson's explicit statements. Changes in the level of public support, in his account, are dominated by the actions of the *least* informed. Stimson tells us (1976: 9), "lack of information about and interest in public policy does not prevent the ill-informed and unattached from evaluating its result. No measurable attention to public affairs is required to know whether times are good or bad, or whether the nation is at war. Similarly, to understand *promised* results requires no attention to policy debates." Stimson assumes that the presence of information means that even the least informed and most inattentive will get the point. Perhaps he is correct, but surely if the least informed and most inattentive are affected by the gap between promise and performance, other things equal, better informed and more attentive Americans will also be affected, and to a greater extent. To argue otherwise requires the assumption that those who pay more attention to politics are more cynical about promises and have no expectations about performance. Stimson offers no evidence to support this assumption.

Why then does Stimson offer this gloomy view of the dynamics of support for the president? I believe the view is offered to undergrid the hypothesis that no matter what presidents attempt, no matter whether they succeed or fail, public support is likely to fade and continue to fade the longer they are in office or until they begin to prepare to seek reelection.

It cannot be denied that presidents tend to lose support over the course of their terms, but this fact does not establish the validity of Stimson's model of public opinion formation. Indeed, any and all phenomena that accrue through time could as well be substituted for Stimson's. Any inexorable process is a

candidate for explaining an inexorable decline in support. Of
course a boundless variety of consistent explanations leaves us
where we began. With only observations of the phenomenon
itself, it is impossible to choose the best explanation. Stimson
offers no evidence to support his model[1] apart from the time
series itself, and since the model asks us to make unreasonable
assumptions about the public, we can set it aside.

Some of the same problems are found in Mueller's (1973)
explanation of the dynamics of presidential support. For Mueller the decline is no less inevitable, but the president is implicated in the process. Mueller labels the process "The Coalition
of Minorities" and describes it as a buildup of negative opinion
from the "gradual alienation" of issue publics.

> "An administration, even if it always acts with majority sup-
> port on each issue, can gradually alienate . . . minorities . . .
> [until] the minority on each issue feels so intensely about its
> loss that it is unable to be placated by administration support
> on other policies that it favors. . . . [T]his concept would pre-
> dict that a president's popularity would show an overall
> downward trend as he is forced on a variety of issues to act
> and thus create intense, unforgiving opponents of former sup-
> porters" (1973: 205).

Under this account, a president cannot win; he can only
lose more or less rapidly. Presumably, the more intensely held
the opinion on an issue and the more nearly equal in size the
groups that prefer one or another policy approach, the higher
the proportion of the public that will move into implacable opposition. In other words, if we order presidents on their degree
of policy initiative, activity, and success—and an unsuccessful
president does not create in an intense issue public the requi-
site sense of loss—we should be able to account for the order of
their rate of decline in aggregate public support.

1. Presser & Converse (1976–77) show that the trends for the better-
educated (arguably the better-informed) compared to the less-well-educated
(arguably the less-informed) do not support Stimson's model.

TABLE 4.1

*Rank-Order Decline in Support in Thirteen
Postwar Presidential Terms*

Presidential term	Average monthly Δ disapproval[a]	Rank	Number of observations
Nixon II	1.93	1	20
Johnson I	1.65	2	7
Truman II	1.05	3	48
Truman I	1.05	4	35
Carter	.93	5	46
Johnson II	.92	6	42
Ford	.69	7	23
Nixon I	.67	8	40
Kennedy	.65	9	34
Reagan II	.23	10	42
Reagan I	.19	11	48
Eisenhower I	.06	12	35
Eisenhower II	.00	13	46

SOURCE: Gallup *Opinion Index*, Report 182, and subsequent reports.

[a] The coefficient is the slope obtained by regressing percent "disapprove" on month in office. "Disapprove" is used to avoid the honeymoon plateau in "approval."

Table 4.1 reports the ordering of thirteen postwar presidential terms by the rate at which public support declined in an average month.[2] President Nixon's second term and President Johnson's first term are ranked at the top. Support in these two presidencies fell away at nearly two percentage points each month on the average. At the other extreme, the two Eisenhower terms show no erosion in support. The nine remaining presidential terms show average losses in the neighborhood of one percentage point per month. The point to consider is whether the ranking in Table 4.1 squares with a reasonable account of successful presidential activism. Is it reasonable to

2. These estimates are drawn from the regression of "percent disapproval" on month in office, $\%\text{DISAP} = a + \beta\,\text{MONTH} + \varepsilon$. The estimates are subject to specification error because rally point effects are not taken into account. However, Mueller (1973: 224) does not use administration-specific rally point estimates; under his procedure, the rank-ordering would be invariant. Kernell (1978: 522) reports administration-specific rally coefficients but does not use the "coalition of minorities" variable. Specification error is more damaging in a relatively short period, such as the Ford presidency, than over the course of a full four years.

hold with the logic of Mueller's position that the Nixon (II) and Johnson (I) presidencies were punished for their policy activism while Eisenhower profited from policy passivity?

We should have no difficulty in agreeing that President Johnson's first term exhibited a high degree of activism in both domestic and foreign policy. However, ranking the second Nixon term ahead and the Eisenhower years behind all other presidential terms in policy activism is not a judgment that will be widely shared. On the contrary, the consensus is that the second Nixon term was distinguished by a paralysis of presidential policy leadership. "Watergate" dominated presidential attention and, arguably, dominated public evaluations of presidential performance as well. The consensus on the activism of the Eisenhower Administration is being reformulated (Greenstein 1982), but those who would accept the Mueller account of opinion formation have the burden of demonstrating that President Eisenhower was noticeably less active than President Nixon in his first term or Presidents Ford, Carter, or Kennedy.

If the Mueller account is misleading on the impact of presidential activism on the dynamics of presidential popularity, perhaps his account of the "implacability" of special-interest hostility (once aroused) is also in error? "Implacability" at the individual level means that once a citizen concludes that presidential performance is below par, he or she will not alter this conclusion. At the level of the aggregate public, "implacability" means that a president's support will erode over the course of the term and not rebound unless an international crisis provides the basis for a rally.

Statistically, "implacability" would mean that a *linear* approximation of the actual data series would be the best we could obtain *using "time" as the single estimator.* This is demonstrably not the case for all of the postwar terms except three—President Kennedy's term, Johnson's brief first term and the second Reagan term. Stimson (1976) has shown that a quadratic estimation is superior to a linear one for the presidential

TABLE 4.2

*Approval Rates in Thirteen Postwar
Presidential Terms: A Comparison of the
Fit of Linear and Quadratic Models*

	Product-moment correlations	
Presidential term	Best linear model	Quadratic model
Truman I	.38	.62
Truman II	.79	.90
Eisenhower I	.09	.55
Eisenhower II	.02	.31
Kennedy	.89	.90[a]
Johnson I	.96	.98[a]
Johnson II	.89	.93
Nixon I	.77	.94
Nixon II	.89	.98
Ford	.43	.70
Carter	.79	.86
Reagan I	.09	.87
Reagan II	.53	.54[a]

SOURCES: Truman I and II, Eisenhower I and II, Kennedy, Johnson II, and Nixon I—Stimson 1976: 12. All other data calculated by the author.

NOTE: "Best linear model" is obtained by regressing relative approval [AP] on time, $AP = \alpha + \beta$ YEARS IN OFFICE $+ \varepsilon$. The "quadratic model" is estimated by regressing relative approval on the difference between the time of the poll and the time point at which approval is minimized (*i.e.*, the "focal" point F). The equation for this model is $AP = \alpha + \beta (\text{F} - \text{YEARS IN OFFICE})^2 + \varepsilon$.

[a]Improvement over "best linear model" is not statistically significant.

terms from Truman's first through Nixon's second. As Table 4.2 shows, a parabolic function of time is superior for the data for the Ford, Carter, and first Reagan terms as well. With only "time" considered we find evidence of a leveling-off and even a recovery of support for the president toward the end of the term. Whatever else this may signify, it does not indicate "implacable" opposition. In Mueller's terms, these trends show that "issue partisans" (Re Pass 1971) may be moved to express disapproval when their preferred option is defeated but that the shift is not necessarily permanent. Disapprovers can change their opinions and again become approvers of presidential performance.

Presidents cannot control time. If time alone depletes the stock of presidential support, then a president's ability to shape public policy is diminished by a force beyond his control. The crux of the matter is "inevitability": Stimson and Mueller argue that the decline is inevitable, but their arguments are demonstrably flawed. The decline is not inevitable and inexorable, but we still do not know why it occurs when it does. This investigation of time and presidential popularity reduces the plausibility that the flow of aggregate opinion on presidential performance is wholly non-substantive. It does not point to the likely substance of the judgment. This is the matter considered in the next four chapters.

CHAPTER 5

Economic Performance and Presidential Popularity

THE FEDERAL GOVERNMENT IS involved in all aspects of the American economy, and the president has a great
deal to say about the shape and depth of that involvement.
More than one-fourth of all American workers depend directly
or indirectly on government expenditures, so that federal employment policy and the budget affect the level of employment
and unemployment. Federal transfer payments are a significant
component of Gross National Product (8.4 percent in 1979, for
example), and policies relating to Social Security, Medicare,
AFDC, and food stamps, for example, affect the growth of the
economy. In total, federal spending amounts to about 20 percent of GNP. In other words, federal government purchases,
taxes, pensions, payrolls, and borrowing unavoidably affect the
state of the economy, and the performance of the economy has
a direct material impact upon all of us (Case 1981: 97–119).

Because the president is the nation's chief policymaker, it
would be reasonable and just if the state of the economy figured prominently in the public's evaluation of presidential job
performance; indeed, it would be perverse and puzzling if it did

not. The expectation of such a linkage has accordingly spawned a substantial body of research.[1] The findings of this research are often contradictory and confusing (if not confused). Happily, the most recent work brings a substantial measure of good political sense to bear and helps clarify the nature of the relationship of the performance of the economy to the public's evaluation of the president's handling of his job.

Douglas Hibbs (1982) finds that indicators of macroeconomic performance—such as unemployment and real income growth rates—have relatively small effects on performance evaluation in the short run. However, "if sustained for two years (eight quarters) or longer, the political penalties and rewards generated by movements in the economy . . . are sizeable" (Hibbs 1982: 328). Hibbs finds further that the public is not of one mind in its responses to macroeconomic outcomes. The six Americans in ten who consider themselves "Democrats" or "Independents"[2] are indifferent between offsetting movements in the rates of unemployment and inflation. In other words, in these political groups opinion of the president's job performance is unlikely to change if sustained rises in inflation are offset by equal and compensating declines in unemployment. With those who think of themselves as "Republicans"— nearly four-tenths of the voting population—the situation is different. Republicans are much more sensitive to inflation than unemployment. In order for a president to maintain his support among Republican partisans, a sustained one percentage point rise in inflation would have to be offset by a four percentage point decline in unemployment.

Hibbs has also examined the response of occupation groups to economic outcomes. He finds that "compared to white-collar workers or those outside the labor force, the political

1. Monroe 1984 and Paldam 1981 organize and present clearly a research literature that is often contradictory in its conclusions.
2. New York *Times*/CBS News Poll, Oct. 18–22, 1987. This figure includes "independents" who think of themselves as "closer" to one or the other major party as partisans.

support of blue-collar workers is more responsive to the economy's real performance than to its nominal, inflation performance" (*ibid.*: 327). Blue-collar workers are not indifferent between rates of inflation and unemployment, but their surplus aversion to inflation is only two-thirds that of white-collar workers and a scant 20 percent that of those outside the labor force. The very substantial aversion to inflation of the 23 percent of the voting population outside the labor force—retirees, housewives, and students—means that a sustained one percentage point increase in unemployment will not erode their support for the president if it is offset by a sustained one-seventh percentage point drop in inflation. By contrast, blue-collar workers' support for the president will erode unless a one percentage point increase in unemployment is accompanied by more than a two-thirds of a percentage point drop in inflation. Overall the public is about twice as inflation-averse as unemployment-averse when sustained policy effects are considered.

Hibbs's findings appear to have important consequences for the dynamics of opinion during Democratic administrations as distinguished from Republican ones. It is commonly believed that Democratic presidents have been willing to let inflation rise in order to promote fuller employment. Republican presidents, by this account, are in accord with their fellow partisans: they are more averse to inflation than unemployment and appear to be willing to use recession as a check on inflation. If this account is accurate, the public's response to macroeconomic outcomes would tend to be advantageous to Republican presidents, relative to Democratic ones, in holding public support. But is the account accurate?

Figure 5.1 provides an answer: If Democratic presidents have tried to reduce unemployment, individually and collectively they have tended to succeed, up to a point. In the average year when a Democrat was in the White House, unemployment dropped one-sixth of a percentage point. Unemployment

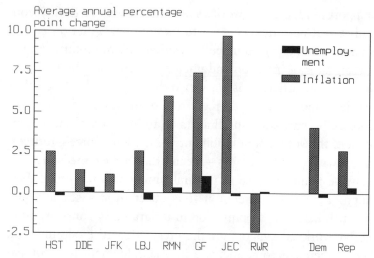

Figure 5.1. Macroeconomic Outcomes in Eight Presidencies.

dropped in three of the four postwar Democratic presidencies, but only the average during Johnson's five years is reliably different from zero (Mean = −0.42; N = 5; t = −2.70; $P_t \leq .025$). The other Democratic presidencies and the overall Democratic average are not significantly different from zero (Mean = −0.21; N = 16; t = −0.73). By contrast, unemployment rose in each of the four postwar Republican presidencies. On the average, about a third of a percentage point of unemployment was added each year with a Republican president in the White House, but this rise is not reliably different from zero (Mean = .35; N = 20; t = 1.10). The half of a percentage point spread between changes in the rate of unemployment in an average year under the two parties is unlikely to be a statistical fluke (Δ = .35; df = 34; t = 1.31; $P_t \geq .10$).

The Democrats may succeed in controlling unemployment, but this success is rarely large enough to offset the public's aversion to inflation. In only four of the 64 quarters that a Democrat has held the White House since the start of Truman's full term in 1949 has unemployment come down twice as fast as inflation rose; Republican presidents brought it off in five of their 80 quarters (through Reagan's first term). This break-even ratio has never been sustained for four quarters, let alone eight. In other words, unemployment rates are simply too sluggish to offset the effects of inflation on public support for the president.

There is certainly nothing sluggish about inflation, but neither is it exclusively a problem for Democratic presidents. On average, inflation has risen just over four percentage points in a year with a Democrat in the presidency. But inflation has gone up a statistically indistinguishable 2.63 percentage points, on average, during the twenty postwar years with Republican presidents in the White House ($\Delta = 1.46$; df $= 34$; t $= 1.05$; $P_t \geq .10$). Figure 5.1 makes it apparent that inflation attaches not to a single party but to an entire era (Case 1981). Of all the postwar presidencies only the Reagan years display negative growth in inflation. President Reagan's first term is unique in another respect: all other recent presidents were less successful than their predecessors in controlling the growth of inflation.

A more detailed look at the data makes clear the change: in thirteen of the 48 quarters between 1949-I and 1960-IV inflation showed a decline; after that, until the Reagan presidency, inflation grew. Moreover, from the end of 1960 until 1981 the size of the growth increased steadily. For each of the four occupants of the White House prior to Reagan, inflation increased ever faster. The growth of inflation in the average year of the Carter Administration was orders of magnitude larger than in the Kennedy Administration. Clearly not all this growth in inflation affects the public's evaluation of the president. President Carter's loss of approval was not orders of magnitude greater than President Kennedy's. But it may well be the case that inflation was a more important ingredient in President Carter's job rating than it was in President Kennedy's. Before we can consider this possibility we must decide on a plausible model of the linkage between the economy and the president's performance ratings.

The Economy and Public Opinion

Stated as extreme simplifications, there are two distinct ways
the performance of the economy can affect public opinion. One
is in its direct effects upon people. Economic trends are virtually unique among policy consequences in this regard—for example, when food prices rise, we all pay more for food. Given
the direction of the impact and the role of the government in
the economy, simple logic dictates that performance judgments
should be related to the personal impact of the economy. The
central hypothesis under the direct effects model is that the
more the individual is affected by the performance of the economy, the more closely tied will his or her evaluation of presidential job handling be to the performance of the economy.
This hypothesis would predict that people who share economic circumstances—for example, the poor, or the unemployed, or for that matter the well-to-do—would also share an
opinion of the president's handling of his job. The hypothesis
would further suggest that those who share a common experience with the economy would by virtue of that experience be
set apart from other opinion-holders. Rising food prices affect
all of us, but those who spend a larger proportion of their income on food are more affected than those who spend less. Unemployment means much more to the unemployed, the families of the unemployed, or fellow workers in industries that are
laying off than it does to those whose employment is secure. In
a word, this model holds that since we are *participants* in the
economy, we are sensitive to its performance and judge the
president—as chief economic policymaker—according to how
we are personally affected.

The second way the performance of the economy can affect
public opinion is spelled out in a model that places the citizen
in the role of *spectator*. Under this model the economy is not a
unique area of policy. It is like other policy areas (foreign policy, military policy, welfare policy, and so forth) in which direct

personal experience is much less widespread. Under this construction, the central hypothesis follows these lines: "Irrespective of personal circumstances and experiences, a failing economy will be reflected in negative presidential job ratings, a succeeding economy in positive ratings."[3]

Such evidence as we have weighs more heavily in favor of the spectator model. This would mean, for example, that one does not have to experience unemployment directly for it to affect one's judgment of presidential performance, and that personal experience with unemployment need not affect one's performance judgments.

We can look more closely at unemployment to illuminate the process. Personal experience can be irrelevant to public opinion either because it is not seen by the individual as "that important" or because it is not believed to be politically relevant. There is no question of unemployment being unimportant to the unemployed. By all accounts the experience is a deep personal tragedy—no less so now, when the financial impact is cushioned by a variety of public programs, than it was in the 1930's when the financial impact was devastating (Schlozman & Verba 1979). But the political relevance of unemployment appears to come from the belief that government is a legitimate source of assistance with problems, and that belief does not appear to be widespread. Those not working are more likely than the public at large to express this belief, but the differences are not large—those holding it representing less than half of the unemployed and being primarily those over the age of 60 (Sniderman & Brody 1977: 508).

If a citizen believes that his or her personal problems should be solved by private means, with personal or family resources, and that government is not a legitimate source of aid, the problem, no matter how intensely experienced, is politically inert

3. A version of this model offers the asymmetric hypothesis that presidents lose support when the economy does poorly but do not profit from a healthy or improving economy. See, for example, Mueller 1973: 213–16.

(Brody & Sniderman 1977; Sniderman & Brody 1977). The fact that the individual directly participates in the problem does not guarantee, or even make likely, the politicization of the problem. To some degree everyone experiences rising prices, but relatively few convert this experience into politically meaningful opinions and behavior (Kinder & Kiewiet 1979; Kinder & Kiewiet 1981; Kinder & Mebane 1982; Kiewiet 1983).

The information taken in by the citizen in the role of *spectator* is already politicized. It comes to the individual through the mass media in the form of information about what government is doing. As a general rule, the more government activity, especially presidential activity, in a given policy area, the more media attention it receives. Media attention shapes public interest (Iyengar & Kinder 1987; MacKuen 1981) and defines the areas in which presidential performance is judged.

To an unknown degree, the government, the media, and consequently the public may be responding to indicators of the performance of the macroeconomy in a patterned sequence. These indicators alert government to the need for corrective action. If the problem is sufficiently serious, political elites will become engaged in corrective attempts. Since to an overwhelming extent "news" entails media reports of elite activity (Gans 1979), elite engagement in the steering of the economy will signal the media that the economy is "news." Stories about the "problem" and government attempts to correct it will migrate from the business pages to the front pages of newspapers and from the middle of television news programs to the top of the show. From the front page and the leading television news stories come the public's sense of the problems facing the nation (MacKuen 1981).

This sequence models the manner in which the macroeconomy gets on the public agenda. If it approximates reality, it alerts us to two important possibilities: if government activity and media attention intervene between the economy and the policy areas to which the public attends, then (1) the mix of attended areas will shift with government activity, and (2) different presidents will be judged on their performance in handling a different mix of problems.

Entailed in this model is the possibility that one or another indication of the performance of the macroeconomy may not figure in the mix of problems on which a given president is judged. If two problem areas are negatively related, the modeled sequence gives rise to the further possibility that the successful handling of one problem may simply shift attention to the other. Thus, if it is true that Democratic presidents are prone to use inflation to reduce unemployment and Republican presidents seek to control inflation with recession and increased unemployment, the strategies may be self-defeating. The successful achievement of one macroeconomic goal may serve to shift public attention to the new problem as it arises.

Regressions of "disapproval" of presidential job performance on indicators of macroeconomic performance for the ten presidential terms from 1949 to 1985 show both these processes at work.[4] Table 5.1 reports the bivariate regression of monthly "disapproval" figures on inflation and unemployment.[5] The results are striking. For the four Democratic presidential terms, unemployment has the wrong sign. Taken at face value, these results would indicate that disapproval of Democratic presidents shrinks as unemployment grows and grows as unemployment shrinks. Inflation, by contrast, has the expected sign during three Democratic administrations. Only in President Truman's second term was inflation unrelated to public support; Presidents Kennedy, Johnson, and Carter all lost ground in their performance ratings as a result of inflation.

4. "Disapproval" is used in order to avoid the "honeymoon" plateaus in approval.

5. Bivariate regression gives a clearer picture of the relationships of macroeconomic indicators to "approval" than does multivariate regression. Unemployment and inflation are to some extent collinear (generally negatively); only the Truman and Kennedy administrations escape sizable collinearity. In the face of this problem, multivariate regression is apt to cloud the conceptual clarity we seek.

TABLE 5.1
*Inflation, Unemployment, and Disapproval of
Presidential Job Handling*

Presidential term	Regression statistics				
	a	b	t_b	R^2	r_{iu}
Truman II	48.4	−0.11(I)	−0.21	.04	.05
	79.3	−7.70(U)	−5.62*	.54	
Eisenhower I	18.0	−0.57(I)	−0.98	.00	−.37
	4.2	3.02(U)	5.82†	.49	
Eisenhower II	24.4	−0.16(I)	0.51	.02	−.32
	6.7	3.18(U)	5.75†	.42	
Kennedy	15.4	0.90(I)	1.44	.03	−.11
	66.7	−8.40(U)	−4.99*	.42	
Johnson	29.5	1.73(I)	2.34†	.10	−.35
	122.2	−21.84(U)	−8.61*	.64	
Nixon I	38.0	−2.12(I)	−3.35*	.21	−.54
	−10.2	7.83(U)	12.21†	.79	
Nixon II	57.5	−0.45(I)	−2.28*	.18	−.87
	−30.1	16.73(U)	3.52†	.38	
Ford	50.6	−2.00(I)	−6.36*	.54	−.69
	−14.0	6.56(U)	5.82†	.49	
Carter	25.3	1.31(I)	3.85†	.13	−.35
	79.5	−6.46(U)	−3.07*	.09	
Reagan I	44.8	−1.08(I)	−4.71*	.22	−.39
	−14.2	6.17(U)	13.83†	.71	

NOTE: Inflation (I) is indexed by the monthly annualized percentage change in CPIW (1967 = 100); unemployment (U) is the rate for all civilian workers; "disapproval" is the average for a given month on the Gallup Poll measure of job approval; "r_{iu}" is the zero-order correlation between the monthly figures on inflation and unemployment. An asterisk (*) indicates that the ratio of the regression coefficient "b" to its standard error (i.e., "t_b") is statistically significant at the α = .05 level but with an incorrect sign. A dagger (†) indicates that the ratio of the regression coefficient "b" to its standard error (i.e., "t_b") is statistically significant at the α = .05 level.

Exactly the opposite situation obtains with a Republican in the White House. In the six Republican presidential terms, inflation shows the perverse relationship with disapproval, and negative job ratings tend to increase with unemployment.

How can it be that to the extent presidents achieve their ends—Democrats reducing unemployment and Republicans controlling inflation—the public responds in such a perverse fashion? The answer, of course, lies with the "unsolved" or remaining macroeconomic problem and the negative relationship between rates of inflation and unemployment. These negative correlations for nine of these ten terms indicate that, to some extent, one macroeconomic problem is handled at the expense of the other. If the opposition political elite makes a point of this (as is their wont) and the media report the opposition's critique of the president's "success" (as they are bound to do), public attention may shift to the unsolved problem area where presidential performance looks less successful. We shall return to this point after considering other aspects of Table 5.1.

In addition to the clear party differences, Table 5.1 indicates trends in the effects of inflation and unemployment on the president's standing with the public. Inflation is not significantly related to negative evaluations of Democratic presidential performance until the Johnson presidency. The slope coefficient (β) is almost certainly zero for Truman's second term. This is to say that knowledge of the level of inflation—for example that it was zero in January 1950 or 19 percent a year later—gives us no knowledge of the likely level of negative evaluation of his performance. During the Kennedy presidency inflation become a factor, albeit a very small one. The regression coefficient $(\beta = .9; t = 1.44; .10 \leq P_t \leq .05)$ has the proper sign but is barely reliably different from zero by the conventional statistical criteria. Inflation was negligible during Kennedy's presidency; in twenty of his 35 months there was no inflation at all, in only four months did it go above an annualized level of 3 percent, and it never reached as high as 7 percent. Small wonder it figured so minimally in his performance ratings.

In the Johnson and Carter administrations the situation is different: inflation affects both these presidents' job ratings, and to about the same degree.[6] Despite the fact that inflation was on average three times higher during Carter's term than during Johnson's—9.9 percent in the average month in the Carter years compared with 3.1 percent in the Johnson years $(\Delta = 6.8\%, t = 10.20; df = 130; P_t \leq .005)$—the effect of inflation on disapproval is about the same.

6. The regression coefficient for inflation in the Johnson presidency is a third larger than in the Carter presidency, but applying statistical criteria, we cannot reject the hypothesis that the two slopes are parallel $(t = 0.42; P_t < .25)$.

Over the postwar years the impact of inflation on the public's perception of Democratic presidents' job performance has steadily increased. The R^2 statistic, which measures the percent of variation in disapproval attributable to inflation, has grown from zero in the Truman and Kennedy terms to 13 percent in the Carter presidency. But even in the Carter term, the bulk of the variation in disapproval (87 percent) remains unaccounted for by the performance of the macroeconomy. For Democratic presidents inflation has become a—not *the*—determinant of their job performance ratings. But even headline-making, runaway inflation leaves a great deal out of the account.

Republican presidents are different from Democratic presidents not only in the measure of macroeconomic performance that affects their job ratings (unemployment versus inflation) but also in the degree to which these ratings are affected by the macroeconomy. Unemployment is a much more important factor in the evaluation of Republican presidents than inflation is for Democratic presidents. The R^2 statistics for the Republicans show between 40 and 80 percent of the variation in disapproval accounted for by rates of unemployment.[7] It is interesting that President Reagan's approval ratings are completely unremarkable in this respect; as with the Republican presidents who preceded him, unemployment is an important determinant of his level of support.

Even if we leave the second Nixon Administration out of the account because of uncertainty over the effect of Watergate, it is obvious that between the Eisenhower years and the Nixon years the impact of unemployment on the public's evaluation of Republican presidents' job performance changed to a marked degree. In the Eisenhower years a one percentage point increase in unemployment, on average, produced a three percentage

7. The first Nixon term exhibits a high degree of serial correlation in measures of both disapproval and unemployment; the second Nixon term shows high serial correlation in disapproval but only moderate serial correlation ($r_{tu} = .67$) in unemployment. For the Eisenhower and Ford presidencies the degree of serial correlation for unemployment is quite low.

point increase in disapproval. After 1968 the effect more than doubled; a one percentage point increase in unemployment produced a six to seven percentage point increase in disapproval.[8]

To summarize: for eight of the ten postwar presidential terms examined, some measure of the performance of the macroeconomy is related to the level of disapproval expressed about the way the president is handling his job. But the analyses make plain that the effects of the economy on the public's response to the president are highly differentiated. Republican presidents are held to account for performance in a different area of the economy than are Democratic presidents. The effects have gotten stronger for recent presidencies than they were in past presidencies. This increase in the significance of economic factors notwithstanding, economic performance is only part of the explanation of the dynamics of presidential popularity.

The president's level of job approval is related to but not fully accounted for by indicators of the performance of the macroeconomy. Over the course of a presidential term the economy may be a factor in producing public approval or disapproval, but the analysis in this chapter and the work of other scholars give every indication that it is only one among many factors that the public brings to its judgment of the president. It is to the attempt to measure the other factors that we now turn.

8. The two Eisenhower slopes are parallel to each other and significantly less steep than the Nixon, Ford, or Reagan slopes.

CHAPTER 6

Daily News and the Dynamics of Support for the President

THE PASSAGE OF TIME *per se* and the performance of the macroeconomy are, respectively, inadequate and incomplete explanations of the dynamics of support for the American president. The interpretations of "time" offered by Mueller and Stimson require us to accept views of the American public that are implausible and, in the cases of Presidents Eisenhower and Reagan, unworkable.[1] By contrast, measures of the performance of the macroeconomy relate in plausible ways to the dynamics of public support for the president and help us understand the role played by the outcomes of public policy in the public's judgment of presidential performance. But in no study—no matter how sophisticated the econometrics employed—does the link between the economy and evaluations of the president justify the conclusion that we need pursue the question no fur-

1. "Time" is not an explanation because any series monotonic with time (e.g., cumulative casualties, the cost of living index, the length of time the president is in office, or even the age of the president) could be a causal factor but undetectable—or indistinguishable from any other factor monotonic with time—when "time" is entered into the equation. See Hibbs 1972 and Kernell 1978.

ther. After a thorough investigation of this relationship, Hibbs concludes (1987: 168) that the impact of macroeconomic performance on the dynamics of support for the president leaves much to be explained. He also states that taking account of "political factors"—primarily, the Vietnam War and Watergate—does not eliminate the need for further research.

The partial success of macroeconomic performance as an explanation of presidential support suggests the direction that the search for a fuller explanation should take. At base, the macroeconomic model assumes (1) that the public takes in evidence of good or bad policy performance (in this case, economic performance), (2) judges the performance against a reasonable standard, and (3) evaluates the president accordingly.[2] To be sure, it may not be fair that the president is judged on outcomes in a policy area in which government policies may in fact have had little impact. But fairness is a different question, one that should be pursued in the psychology of attributions of cause and blame. A fuller explanation of the dynamics of public support needs to apply this model to non-economic policy areas as well as to the area of economic policy.

The underlying logic of the model of the evaluation of macroeconomic performance is not without its problems, and these problems are, if anything, more evident when we expand the scope of the policy areas in which presidential performance is evaluated. Answers to the following three questions are essential to a grounded, fuller explanation of the dynamics of support for the president. First, in which areas of activity is evidence of presidential success or failure sought by the public?

2. Peffley and Williams (1985) argue that the attribution of blame is a necessary condition for the political impact of any public policy failure. They point to President Reagan's ability to blame President Carter and the Democrats in Congress for the recession of 1982 as the reason he escaped its negative effect on his popularity. Adams (1984), by contrast, provides evidence that President Reagan was *not* able to escape the negative consequences of the recession of 1982. Peffley and Williams may be wrong in the specifics, but that does not gainsay the importance of understanding the process of attribution of blame or praise. This is a question I will address at length below.

What draws the public's attention to these areas? Is it useful to conceive of a "baseline" policy area and then model attention to other policy areas as "diversions" from the baseline? In other words, what drives the dynamics of policy salience for the public? Second, by what standard is policy performance judged? The basic alternatives are the individual's private standard and shared standards. If evaluation is a product of the match between expectation and outcome, what are the sources of public expectations for policy outcomes? Third, assuming that individuals do not change their opinion of presidential performance from instant to instant—which is to assume that public opinion has an inertial component (Brody & Page 1975; Kernell 1978)—how should we model the dynamic and inertial components of public opinion?

In the balance of this chapter, these questions will be used to guide the development of a fuller model of the dynamics of support for the president, to suggest operational procedures for testing the model, and to set the stage for examining the model with data on presidential approval from 1961 (Kennedy) through 1984 (the first Reagan term).

Salient Public Policies: The Ingredients of Evaluation

On any given day, the world produces innumerable events which, in principle, could affect the opinion of the president held by Americans. Of course, most of these events are simply unknown to any or all Americans and cannot either reinforce or change the collective view of the president held by the public. The world of potentially relevant events is radically simplified for any given citizen by a lack of exposure to the event. Those events that are brought to the individual's attention often lack relevance for his or her evaluation of presidential performance. In this area, as in most areas of attitude formation and change, the "attention" and "comprehension" mediators stand as screens between the individual and a complex world of information (McGuire 1968).

Some events are directly experienced by individual citizens, require no mediation, and are potential ingredients of the process of evaluation. For these events, the individual's "comprehension of political relevance,"—i.e., the perception of a link between the experience and the political system—determines whether or not the event will be part of the evaluation process. However, the screening out of potentially relevant events is not entirely volitional. Most of the world, if known at all, is known vicariously, through the media of mass communication. Consequently, the norms and routines of media "gatekeeping" affect whether events will become ingredients of the evaluation process (MacKuen 1981; Behr & Iyengar 1982). The political relevance of direct personal experience and the processes of media gatekeeping have been carefully studied; from this research we can draw a plausible picture of the process by which events become the ingredients of evaluation.

By and large, personal experiences have been found to be politically irrelevant. Brody and Sniderman (1977) found that three Americans in four do not believe that government is a source of relief for their "most important personal problem." They also found that personal problems are politically relevant for only those Americans who believe that government ought to help solve their most pressing problem; most Americans are in this respect "self-reliant" (Brody & Sniderman 1977). Feldman adds to our understanding of the general irrelevancy of personal problems by rooting the phenomenon in the ideology of "individualism" (1982). Personal problems—and by extension, personal experiences—despite their acknowledged salience for the individual, do not appear to be the basic ingredients of performance evaluation for most Americans.

What is true of personal experiences in general is also true of economic experiences in particular. Schlozman and Verba (1979) studied the political impact of personal experience with unemployment and found that in the depression of the 1930s and in the recession of the early 1970s, personal experience with unemployment was not particularly politically potent. The unexpected political inertness resulting from wrenching personal experience Schlozman and Verba attribute to a persistent hope that conditions will improve and a continuing belief in the "American Dream" (1979: 140). Kinder and Kiewiet (1979; see also Kinder 1981) find that personal economic experiences, in general, lack political cogency for the citizen. In their view, the linking of measures of macroeconomic performance with measures of presidential popularity reflects judgments of how the incumbent is handling national economic problems and is not a projection of the citizen's own economic satisfaction or discontent (Kinder & Kiewiet 1979: 523).[3]

From this review of past research it is plausible to conclude that personal experiences and problems will not be, for most Americans, a central ingredient of the evaluation process. This means, of course, that, to the extent that the dynamics of popular support for the president represent a process of attitude change, the ingredients of that process will be drawn from vicarious rather than direct experiences. For all intents and purposes, "vicarious" political events are experienced through the media of mass communication and particularly the news.[4]

3. Kramer (1983) challenges this interpretation. He argues that individual-level findings are sensitive to the method of measurement and that neither individual-level nor aggregate data can distinguish whether the citizen is responding to personal or national economic conditions (Kramer 1983: 106). The cogency of Kramer's challenge will inevitably leave us with uncertainty about the ingredients of the evaluation process and also about the standard by which performance is judged. However, Kramer's analysis has itself been challenged (Scicchitano 1984; see also Kramer 1984).

4. This conclusion ignores the process of the "two-step" flow of communication, in which opinion leaders draw information from the mass media and retail it in direct conversation with members of the public (Katz & Lazarsfeld 1955). Without question such communication takes place, but its relevance for evaluation of presidential performance has not been studied. Indeed, the role of a two-step flow in the current media environment—with the massive presence of network television news—has not been given much thought. For an analysis and critique of the concept, see Janowitz 1968: 51.

For our present purpose, an understanding of the ingredients of the process of evaluation must begin with a review of what is known about what the news media bring to the American public.

The burden of the argument thus far is that, in the main, the public evaluates presidential performance in those policy areas covered by the mass news media. News media attention is a necessary but not a sufficient condition for public attention.[5] The other necessary conditions have to do with relatively enduring individual qualities (such as political interest and sophistication), the correlates of cognitive capacity (such as education, intelligence, and self-esteem, which serve to mediate individual attention to public affairs [McGuire 1968]), and media editorial practices (which signal the public that a particular event is considered to be "very important"). If in the short run individual qualities associated with the attention mediator are stably distributed, the more attention paid by the media to a given topic, the more prominent it will be on the public's agenda, and the more likely it will be that this topic will be an ingredient in the evaluation process. In other words, in the short-term dynamics of presidential support, the editorial practices of the mass news media will be one of the main determinants of the ingredients in the process of evaluation.

Editorial practice uses a variety of techniques for signaling that a story is "important." The makeup of a daily newspaper or a nightly television news program is stylized, and the public

5. Research on the link between media attention and the public's agenda— usually indexed by responses to some variant of the question "what are the most important problems facing the nation?"—draws a distinction between the impact of news and "real world cues" (Erbring, Goldenberg & Miller 1980; MacKuen 1981; Behr & Iyengar 1982). "Real world cues," in this context, mean indications of the performance of the political or economic system as distinguished from news stories about that performance. But this distinction is not relevant to "sociotropic" judgments—evidence of the "real world cues" will be likely to be available to most of the public through the media. The distinction alerts us to the possibility that in some issue areas the media have less room for independence—for journalistic "enterprise"—than in other issue areas.

is familiar with the "code." The media signal importance by display practice—by location within the paper or the show, by the accompanying visual material, by size of headlines, etc. Importance is also signaled by the quantity of attention to the story—by the volume devoted to a story on a given day and by the number of days the story is covered.

Volume of coverage signals importance because news space/time is limited. Nightly television news is presented in a very rigid time frame—the half-hour network broadcasts offer about 22 minutes of news every night.[6] Space in newspapers is not nearly as rigid as time on television, but expansion and contraction of newspaper space have more to do with the weekly cycle of advertising than with the response of the "news hole" to breaking news (Bogart 1981). With total volume more or less fixed, a large fraction devoted to a given story signals the reader/viewer that a topic is worthy of attention.

Attention to a given topic over time is yet another way in which the media direct and redirect the salience of a policy area for the public. To be sure, on some stories the natural rhythms of events determine the duration of press attention. But more often than not, events proceed while press attention flags for lack of a dramatic turn. The number of days or weeks or months devoted to a given topic reflects editorial decisions that collate judgments about the intrinsic importance of the events with organizational considerations, including the availability of staff to file stories.

The question arises whether display, space/time on a given day, and attention over time are fungible from the perspective of affecting the public's agenda. I can find no study that speci-

6. In a 100-day random sample drawn from the Vanderbilt University *Television News Abstracts and Index* for the period 1972 to 1980, the three-network average news hole was 21.92 minutes (SD = 1.24 minutes). On the average day, 14.98 stories were covered (SD = 3.18 stories). There are small but statistically significant inter-network differences: CBS, on the average, has a slightly larger news hole than NBC, and NBC's is slightly larger than ABC's. The means are CBS, 22.6 minutes; NBC, 21.8 minutes; and ABC, 21.4 minutes.

fies substitution ratios for agenda-setting, but given what we know about public attention to politics in general, I would expect coverage over time to be more productive of public attention than either display or volume on a given day. Public inattention to the details of politics is made of resistant material that can be best worn away by persistent exposure. There seems to be little reason to doubt the proposition that the longer a story runs and the more prominence it is accorded by the media, the larger the proportion of the public that will declare it an important national issue. The public's consciousness of the areas in which policy performance is to be judged is, in MacKuen's phrase, a "mediated consciousness" (1981: 118).

The public agenda—at least, the sociotropic agenda—and the ingredients of the evaluation process are determined by the editorial practices of the producers of daily news.[7] The news media focus and frame reality for the public. However, the world they bring to the public is not a world created out of whole cloth; rather, it is a world of real events in which some are selected because in an editor's professional judgment they are believed to be intrinsically important or because it would be professionally embarrassing not to have selected them. Editors frame and focus the public agenda further by distinguishing—and signaling the distinction—between important and very important news. Given what we know about what the public takes away from its exposure to daily news (Neuman 1976),[8] it is reasonable to assume that the main ingredients of

7. Direct, experimental evidence for this proposition is found in the research of Shanto Iyengar, Donald Kinder, and their associates (e.g., Iyengar, Kinder & Peters 1982). Iyengar and Kinder (1987), by increasing the volume of coverage of various news topics, were able to increase the salience of the topic for their experimental subjects and the role of the topic in their subjects' evaluation of the president.

8. Neuman (1976: 119) finds that a sample of the public can recall just over one story (mean = 1.2) from that evening's national television news when contacted within three hours of the broadcast. Viewers can recognize more news stories when they are prompted with headlines—on the average, the number of stories recognized with some details is 4.4 and without details is an additional

public evaluation of presidential performance will be the set of these "very important" news stories.

The news media are the proximal source of the information with which the public deals; in this sense, they set the public agenda. In a broader sense, however, the political elite in general, the president in particular, and the public itself are important participants in the process as well. This is to say that news media may not be invariably the origin of the salience of policy areas independent of other potential sources of public concern about public policy. From recent studies a more complex and contingent process emerges: Erbring, Goldenberg, and Miller conclude, from their study of media in the agenda-setting process, that the issue agenda is affected by news only when "media coverage interacts with the audience's pre-existing sensitivities to produce changes in issue concerns." For them, "issue coverage in the media serves as a trigger" to activate the audience's latent concerns (1980: 45). Behr and Iyengar bring the sensitivities of the political elite into the account; they conclude, from their study of agenda setting, that "[the] public agenda is indeed affected by what television journalists and editors choose to broadcast as news. However, news coverage is not the sole source of citizens' issue concerns. As real world conditions worsen and the president turns his attention to particular issues, public concern for these issues increases" (1982: 21). The complexities introduced by these studies need to be borne in mind. However, as I have said before, although the media do not create the world out of whole cloth, they do select what to cover and how to play it. Even if we acknowledge that the decisions of what to select and how to play it are

---

4.3 stories. Since the average news broadcast, in Neuman's study, had 19.8 stories, depending upon how one classifies the stories respondents claim to recognize but for which they can supply no details, between 50 and 70 percent of the daily evening news is not memorable to the American public. Unfortunately, Neuman does not report whether display prominence—conventionally, the appearance of a story at the "top" of the show, i.e., before the first commercial—affects the likelihood of recall or recognition with detail.

affected by public and elite sensitivities, the importance of the media as the proximal source of the public's agenda makes daily news indispensable to our understanding of the dynamics of public support for the president.

An important implication of this construction of the processes by which a policy area becomes salient for the public is that no policy area serves as a "baseline." We might well expect that when a particular series of events dominates the news over an extended period—such as Vietnam between 1964 and 1970 or Watergate in 1973 and 1974—presidential performance will be judged in the dominant area. But this construction also implies that in "slow news" periods—i.e., times when no one event or group of related events dominates the news—the public does not return to a particular policy area in which to judge presidential performance. Rather than returning to a baseline policy area, the public works with the world as it is presented in the daily news; the mix of policies entering the performance judgment is likely to differ from president to president.

The Standards for Performance Evaluation

The changing mix of events and the consequent shifting focus of public attention from one policy area to another may simplify accounting for the standards used by the public in judging presidential performance. A completely egocentric public—one in which each individual judges presidential performance on the degree of satisfaction with the details of her or his personal life—would make it nearly impossible, and certainly impractical, to account for the aggregate flow of public opinion. With an egocentric public, we would have to determine the relative salience of the individual's life details and his or her satisfaction with those details in order to generate a measure of "net satisfaction" weighted by salience. Considering this task, the rarity of political egocentricity is a welcome convenience. A sociotropic public—one that judges performance on the problems facing the nation—limits the kinds of standards that can be employed.

With respect to "national" (as distinguished from "personal") problems we can make use of Donald Stokes' distinction between "valence" and "position" issues (1966: 170–73) in accounting for the evaluative standards employed by the public.[9] Stokes defines "position" issues as "those that involve advocacy of government action from a set of alternatives over which a distribution of voter preferences is defined" (*ibid.*: 170). Position issues involve the valuing of means (policies) as well as ends. By contrast, "valence" issues are "those that merely involve the linking of the [political] parties with some consequence that is positively or negatively valued by the electorate" (*ibid.*: 170–71). Peace and prosperity are prototypical valence issues; there is no disagreement in the public that they are desirable. Valence issues can be a bit more specific: for example, there is no disagreement in the public or in the elite that sustained inflation and high unemployment are undesirable. Inflation and unemployment are, in this respect, valence issues; they enjoy this status despite the fact that some individuals may be better off with cheaper, inflated money or that inflation may be curbed by reduced wage demands in periods of high unemployment.

There are problems associated with understanding valence issues. Two critical ones are (1) How do issues achieve and retain this status with the public? and (2) What determines the linking of consequences with political figures or institutions? These problems notwithstanding, the standards for performance evaluation associated with valence issues are not

9. Ostrom and Simon use a similar distinction in their account of the dynamics of presidential popularity (1985: 336). They distinguish between outcomes that would be expected of any president and those expected because of the policy agenda of a particular occupant of the White House. The former would include valence issues and the latter presidentially generated position issues. However, it is not clear how Ostrom and Simon handle issues that are put on the president's agenda by other domestic and foreign political elites.

problematic. The question of the evolution of valence issues—
of what Stokes terms the "overwhelming consensus as to the
goal of government action" (*ibid.*: 172)—can be dodged; it is
clearly beyond the scope of this essay. But I cannot dodge the
question of linkage. This is a study of the evaluation of presidential performance and I cannot avoid addressing the question
of why presidents get judged on valence issue performance.
Hopefully, a very brief account will be convincing.

Scholars of the presidency argue for a number of trends in
the evolution of the office over the course of the twentieth century; all of these trends tend to place the president at the focus of national politics. Terms like "imperial presidency" may
obscure more than they clarify and are controversial in detail,
but they also contain a central truth about the president. The
American president has become an extraordinary figure among
the American political elite (Schlesinger 1973). The president
is at the focus of national attention on a day-to-day basis (Gans
1979), and not only in periods of national crisis—as was Lincoln
during the Civil War or Wilson during the First World War. The
evolution of the centrality of the president as a political figure has been paralleled by an expansion of the policy areas in
which the rest of the political elite expects the president to
exercise leadership. Richard Neustadt describes this process as
an expansion of the "clerkship" responsibilities of the office
and characterizes the evolution as "[t]he President now [doing]
routinely what his predecessors innovated, often daringly"
(1982: 3).

Neustadt (1982: 1) details the process as the institution-
alizing of

> a variety of White House ventures more or less unknown
> before this century. These range from central budgeting to
> legislative programming, from labor-disputes settlement to
> macroeconomic "management." *Et cetera.* The list is long
> and growing longer. Each item stems from an *ad hoc* ini-
> tiative once taken by TR or some successor, but now set in

statute or confirmed by custom and continuing, term after term. Characteristically, such things survive because they are perceived by others than the sitting President as useful in the doing of their jobs. Congressmen, officials, staff aides, journalists, and advocates for private interests—all discover their own stakes in institutionalization. So it occurs.

As the president has evolved as the focus of national politics, he has also become the focus of attention of news media coverage (Gans 1979) and, unquestionably, the most prominent political figure to the American public (Greenstein 1965).

It is a very short step to the expectation that these developments in the evolution of the office carry with them benefit and loss for the president in areas where there is a national consensus on the goals of government action—that is to say, on "valence" issues. If the public expects "prosperity" and the news convinces the public that the nation is gaining it, the president will benefit with increased support; otherwise, he will lose support. If the public agrees that "peace" and "security" are desirable and the news carries the impression that peace is in jeopardy and that security is fragile, the president will lose support. Other political figures and institutions may also gain or lose in periods of extended attention to a valence issue. But as the political figure with the greatest volume of news media coverage, the president is most likely to have his evaluation by the public related to flows of valence issue news.[10]

"Position" issues also enter into the judgment of the president, but the differences between the two types of issues mean that we need a separate account of the standards by which performance is judged. On position issues, for both ends and means, there is a division of opinion in the elite and, perhaps,

10. Douglas Hibbs has provided us with the details of the conditions under which two valence issues—inflation and unemployment measured by actual rates—are traded off as "the most important problems facing the nation" (1979). It is my as yet untested contention that if we use media attention to valence issues as our independent variable, we can move beyond "prosperity"—to issues like "corruption" or "pollution"—in studying the flows of valence issues.

in the public as well. In other words, the politicization of position issues is much greater than the politicization of valence issues. Position issues are presented to the public in the form of a policy debate. The effect of politicization on the standards employed by the public is contingent on whether ideology is activated by the policy-related events and on whether preexisting preferences for one side or the other are activated in the policy debate.

"Ideology," in the sense used here, means a distinct preference for a class of policy options. For example, those who routinely look to regulation or to free market solutions are in this sense "ideological." Those who fix responsibility for problems with the individual and those who, by contrast, blame society for the individual's problems both choose policy options on the basis of these views about individual or collective responsibility and so are acting ideologically. For individuals who have ideological predispositions toward a class of policy options, a match between their predisposition and the president's proposal would lead to a positive increment in their evaluation of his performance. A mismatch would lead to a negative increment. Converse describes the linking as follows (1975: 84): "Often such ideological stances are quite explicit: they depend upon highly generalized views as to social causation, the nature of justice, the character of the ideal political order, and the like. Thus if we have knowledge of a person's deeper value premises, we can more or less predict his or her assessments of more discrete and specific issue controversies."

By most accounts, however, few Americans apply ideological tests to policy options (Converse 1975: 84–89). Issue opinions appear to be disconnected from each other.[11] "Morselized"

11. General disconnection and lack of stability are not universally accepted as the state of the issue opinions of most Americans. Norman Nie and his associates have argued that with the appearance of more ideologically specific candidates, such as Goldwater in 1964, the public exhibited more ideological connection between issue opinions (Nie & Anderson 1974; Nie & Rabjohn 1979). This contention has sparked a heated controversy on the com-

is Lane's term for the lack of connection among opinions on issues and between issue opinions and historical or ideological patterns (1962: 353).

For morselized opinions, evaluations could flow from pre-dispositions toward one side of the debate or the other, or from a focus on the unambiguous aspect of the policy which is its manifest result: faced with a debate about policy options, without the guidance of ideology, most members of the public will tend to take the side of those with whom they otherwise identify. As a first approximation, for most purposes in American politics, this means siding with those in the elite who share the citizen's partisan identification.[12] Thus, those who share the president's partisanship should—other things being equal—approve of his policy proposals, and those who share the partisanship of the opposition should side with the opposition against the president. The announcement of a presidential policy proposal should, under this construction, yield a gain in

---

plexity and stability of American public opinion and on the methodological justification for Nie's conclusions (Achen 1975; Sullivan, Piereson & Marcus 1978). The debate ran its course without either side capitulating and, surprisingly, was not given a fresh test with the advent of the Reagan candidacy. Research on policy trade-off reasoning (Shanks et al. 1982) and on the role of ideology in the formation of preferences for public policy toward racial integration (Sniderman, Kuklinski & Brody 1984) tends to indicate that while some Americans can reason from more general principles to policy preferences, most Americans do not.

12. Identifications besides partisanship are conceivably involved in the process of evaluation. Curiously, partisan identifications powerfully affect policy opinions even though they are seldom explicitly invoked in policy debates. Other identifications are frequently invoked in policy debates; consider the frequency with which, for example, "farmers," "working men and women," "consumers," and "the small businessman" are used as symbols for the interests affected by a particular policy option. Participants in the policy process evidently believe that members of the public respond to policy debates framed in terms of these identifications, but little research has been carried out to determine whether this belief is well founded. For examples of studies that look to identifications other than party, see Weatherford 1978; Kline 1984; Kinder 1981. These studies yield a mixed answer to the question of whether identifications with social class, gender, or a group in general affect one's attitude formation.

support from his fellow partisans and a loss in support among opposition partisans. In an aggregate public with a relatively balanced division of partisanship, policy proposals should lead to little net change in approval of presidential job performance. Partisan predispositions, depending upon the balance of partisanship, can lead to aggregate stability in presidential support in periods in which policy proposals dominate the news—this may be one source of the "honeymoon" in the first term. A corollary of this proposition would lead us, in periods in which policy proposals predominate, to expect that performance evaluations disaggregated by partisan identification would show divergent trends, with the president's fellow partisans increasing their level of support—subject to ceiling effects—while opposing partisans withdraw their support.

These propositions follow from the assumption that proposals for solving problems are ambiguous stimuli for most Americans. But the news relevant for performance evaluations is not limited to policy proposals; the public also is given news on the results of policy. The distinction is illustrated, for example, when the president submits a bill to Congress: the submission is a proposal; the subsequent debate will likely involve more proposals; however, when Congress acts it will have produced a result. To be sure, it may be no more than a political result (as distinguished from a policy result), but it is a result nonetheless. On the whole, results news is less ambiguous than proposal news.

The distinction between political and policy results has to do with the system being affected. Suppose that the president wishes to reduce the foreign trade deficit by some tariff manipulation. If Congress accepts or rejects the president's proposal for the tariff manipulation, it will have produced a political result. The factors determining whether Congress accepts the proposal include the president's persuasiveness, counterpressures on Congress, and all the other elements of "presidential power" (Neustadt 1980). If Congress accepts the proposal and the trade deficit fails to respond, a policy result will have occurred—in this example, a negative result. The determinants of policy success or failure have to do with whether the policy is apposite to the causal structure of the system it is designed to change.

By what standards are results judged by the public? Ideology could provide the standard. That is to say, the public could judge positively a positive result from a policy option that is in accord with its ideological preferences and negatively a positive result from an option that was ideologically offensive. But as I have argued before, the limited use of ideological standards by the public and the low probability that a given results story will fall within the scope of a citizen's ideology mean that few Americans will judge policy results in this manner.

Intense concern for a particular policy area could provide the standard. Here my departure from Mueller (1973) is most apparent. Mueller appears to apply a "single-issue" standard: he treats citizens as if they are intense single-issue voters. Once the president has acted contrary to the preference of such citizens on issues about which they care most deeply, their support is irrevocably withdrawn. But there is no evidence that any sizable fraction of the public is, in this sense, ineluctably "single-issue." On the contrary, the capacity of presidents to recover support is an indication that a single-issue standard is not applied in the aggregate.

Partisan predispositions could also provide the standard. But they require elite leadership and the elite finds little profit in quarreling with success. Policy proposals may be the subject of intense elite partisan debate—which instructs partisans in the public—but policy results usually leave silent those in the elite who had predicted the contrary outcome. This silence precludes much of the public from applying a partisan standard in using news of policy results in updating their assessment of presidential performance. Ideology and/or partisanship may have more impact on the evaluation of "political" results than on "policy" results. There is more scope for elite criticism or crowing about outcomes that have yet to be tested in the "real world." Consequently, elite inputs have a greater likelihood of an impact on the public's performance judgment on political results. But elite commentary after the fact does not qualify as "news" for very long and this restricts the effects of criticism and crowing on public opinion.

Under these circumstances, the public responds to news of the outcome of both political and policy processes as if the news concerned valence rather than position issues. As in the case of valence issues, the public judges the results on the standards that the president has set or accepted. When the news reports a result in accord with the expectations set by the president, the public treats that as "good" news and adds a positive increment to its evaluation of the president; when the news media report results that are contrary to presidential expectations, the "bad" news detracts from the public's evaluation of presidential performance.

In summary, the standards by which performance is judged come from the common consensus on issues about which there is little political debate. On these "valence" issues, news reports bring information to the public on progress or the lack of progress toward goals that are not in dispute. The public uses this information in updating its assessment of the president. On "position" issues, the public in the aggregate discounts policy proposals and looks to political and policy outcomes—to "results"—for information on presidential performance. Because the political elite, following its own interests, offers little opinion leadership on policy outcomes, the effects of predispositional standards are muted, and the public tends to judge the president on the standard of the expectations he has set. When results match presidential expectations, the public responds positively; when presidential expectations are not met, the president suffers a loss of support in the public.

Dynamic and Inertial Components
in Support for the President

Commentators on human information-processing express fun-
damentally different viewpoints on the effectiveness of new information in changing the individual's opinions and assessments. Consider, for examples, the views of Sir Francis Bacon
and Ben Bagdikian. Bacon sees little prospect of change: "The
human understanding when it has once adopted an opinion
draws all things else to support and agree with it. And though
there be a greater number and weight of instances to be found
on the other side, yet these it either neglects and despises, or
else by some distinction sets aside and rejects, in order that by
this great and pernicious predetermination the authority of its
former conclusion may remain inviolate" (quoted in Nisbett &
Ross 1980: 167).

Bagdikian is much more hopeful about the possibility of
change if the media are even-handed: "Our picture of reality
does not burst upon us in one splendid revelation. It accumulates day by day and year by year in mostly unspectacular fragments from the world scene, produced mainly by the mass
media. Our view of the world is dynamic, cumulative, and self-
correcting as long as there is a pattern of even-handedness [on
the part of the press] in deciding which fragments are important" (1983: x).

If we apply these insights to the subject of public opinion,
we find these commentators sharing a view of the role of inertia in opinion formation and disputing whether inertia totally
dominates the process. Which side should we choose in this
dispute? Contemporary cognitive psychologists are closer to
Bacon than Bagdikian in their account of "belief perseverance"
(Nisbett & Ross 1980), but they soften Bacon's view of the iron-
clad resistance of opinion to new information. In outline the
process is patterned after "scientific method," but a less than
ideal scientific method. People's understanding and evaluation
of the constant flow of social or political events may depend,

according to Nisbett and Ross, "on a rich store of general knowledge of objects, people, events, and their characteristic relationships. Some of this knowledge may be represented as beliefs or theories, that is, reasonably explicit 'propositions' about the characteristics of objects or object classes" (*ibid.*: 28). The theories can come from a rendering of recent history into clichés or maxims—"the Republicans are the party of hard times" or "the Democrats are the party of war"—or from a characterizing of one political figure by other opinion leaders—"Jimmy Carter is wishy-washy" or "Walter Mondale is the candidate of the special interests"—or from one's political socialization, or from who knows where.

The citizen's theory need not be as simple as these one-liners. However, as I have repeated, most studies find relatively few Americans with a complex, well articulated, interconnected theory of politics. Irrespective of their complexity, these lay theories are "important because they provide an interpretative framework for the lay scientist—one that resolves ambiguity and supplements the information 'given' with much 'assumed' information" (*ibid.*: 29).

Theories persevere because they affect information-processing (*ibid.*: 169): preexisting theories help the individual select relevant information, but information confirming the theory tends to be overselected. If evidence is approached without the benefit of a theory and a theory is formed from this initial evidence, the theory will resist further evidence (*ibid.*: 169–71). If the standard for "scientific" information-processing is that unambiguous data contradicting a theory should force a revision in the theory, most information-processing fails to meet this standard. It is not, as Bacon would have it, that lay theories do not change at all. Rather, psychological experimental evidence points to the conclusion that "generally there has been less change than would be demanded by logical or normative standards or that changes . . . occur more slowly than would result from an unbiased view of the accumulated evidence" (*ibid.*: 189). In other words, cognitive psychologists would reply to Bagdikian that even though the news gatekeepers might be even-handed in giving the fragmented picture of the world to the public, the public's view of the world—however dynamic and cumulative—would be somewhat inaccurate and only grudgingly self-correcting.

We have in the work of the cognitive psychologists and Bagdikian's insight a straightforward account of the "lag structure" that Monroe and other scholars have found to be characteristic of the relationship of macroeconomic indicators to aggregate public support for the president (Monroe 1984). Consider the hypothetical case of a Democratic president and a rise in the Consumer Price Index [CPI]: If the media deem the rise newsworthy and give it prominent coverage, initially some Americans will overselect evidence of wage increases to confirm their belief that "the Democrats are the party of prosperity"; others will overselect evidence of the increase in the cost of living to confirm their belief that "Democrats do not know how to manage the economy" and/or "want to debase the dollar." Eventually, if the rise in the CPI accelerates and "inflation" news moves to the front page and the top of the evening news, the belief of the latter group will be reinforced and the former group's confidence in their theory about Democrats and prosperity will gradually give way to the elite interpretation of the evidence about the performance of the economy. The aggregate result of this process would be the lag structures found in the over-time relationship of the rate of inflation to approval of presidential job performance.

A parallel case for the effect of unemployment on performance evaluations would be easy to construct. More generally, we have in these instances a model of the dynamics of any valence issue that achieves prominence on the public agenda. Predispositions matter in the processing of information on valence issue performance, but the weight of performance-related evidence will eventually erode the beliefs of all but the truest of the "true believers."

This cognitive psychological account can be applied to position issues as well. It has been argued that the public in the aggregate does not have strong predispositions with respect to position issues and derives its expectations about outcomes from the statements of the president (Brody 1982; Ostrom & Simon 1985). In the term employed by cognitive psychologists (Abelson 1976), presidentially set expectations "script" a scenario for the outcome of public policy in light of some policy-relevant action. The script functions as a lay theory of the policy domain. Outcomes consistent with scripted expectations will increase approval of presidential performance through an enhanced belief in the president's competence (Popkin, Gorman, Phillips & Smith 1976). Ambiguous outcomes may not erode perceptions of the president's competence and may actually increase it. The implications of clearly negative results may be resisted by some for a time, but eventually support for the president will decline in the face of evidence that outcomes do not satisfy scripted expectations.

These hypotheses suggest that both inertial and dynamic factors will affect the public's collective impression of presidential performance. The division of public opinion about how well the president is handling his job in any given poll will be a compound of prior impressions of his adequacy and recent information that sheds light on his performance. Given a positive balance to the news reflecting on presidential performance in any given period, we would expect those who already approve of the president's job handling to be reinforced in their assessment and to be joined by some of those who, on balance, in the prior period disapproved of the way in which the president was doing his job. The larger the balance of positive news, the larger will the group be of former disapprovers moving into the ranks of the approvers. Given a negative balance to the news in any given period, we would expect the same process to account for the movement of public opinion in the opposite direction.

Several factors would govern the pace of the movement of

public opinion. First would be the distribution of the initial dispositions to approve or disapprove of the president. Kernell approximates this with the division of partisanship (1978). Second would be the distribution of the degree of certitude with which these predispositions are held—this is a strength of belief or tenacity variable. Third would be the accumulated information reflecting on presidential performance, and last the size of the discrepancy between the information in the current period and the accumulated prior information.

Taken together, these factors form the basic elements of Norman Anderson's information integration theory of attitude dynamics, which was adapted by Brody and Page and Timothy Haight to account for the movement of support for the president (Anderson 1974; Brody & Page 1972; Haight & Brody 1977; Haight 1978: 100–115). The first and second predispositional factors will affect initial levels of support and the impact of ambiguous results on changes in support. The third factor is inertial—it is modeled as the average of information up to the period preceding the current period. Current information is incorporated into this average, and the more discrepant the current information, the more change in support we would expect. However, the incorporation of new information about presidential performance into the accumulation of past information means that the impact of a discrepancy of a given size on public opinion will vary with when it occurs in a presidential term; in other words, the variance of public support should decline as the term progresses unless the magnitude of discrepancy becomes ever more extreme (Haight 1978: 110).

Testing the Information Integration Model

In essence the model detailed in the preceding sections hypothesizes (1) that the evaluation of presidential performance will be determined by reports that carry information on the meeting of goals for which there is a consensus in the polity and/or reports relevant to the expectations of policy outcomes that the president has set for the nation; (2) that public attention to a given issue area will be determined in the main by the quantity and quality of news coverage; (3) that results—rather than proposals—will be the basic ingredient of the evaluation;[13] and (4) that the information in current reports of policy results will be combined with past reports of results to determine the direction and amount of opinion change.

Detailed descriptions of our operational procedures have been published elsewhere (Stone & Brody 1970; Brody & Page 1972; Haight 1978) so that in the present context a sketch of these procedures should be sufficient:

Dependent Variable. Our measure of the evaluation of presidential performance is supplied by responses to the Gallup Poll question: "Do you approve or disapprove of the way [NAME OF THE INCUMBENT] is handling his job as president?" For the most part in the analyses that follow, the dynamics of "approval" percentage will be the object of study. We have done parallel analyses of "disapproval" with essentially similar results—which is not surprising since the two time series are the mirror image of each other after the first six months of the first term.

In recent years other polling organizations have also tracked public support for the incumbent with this or a similar item, but the Gallup organization [American Institute of Public Opinion, AIPO] has conducted in-person interviews with the same

13. Up to this point, our model and the Ostrom and Simon model (1985) are basically similar. Beyond this point, however, they differ in two fundamental respects. First, the model proposed here hypothesizes that impressions based upon new information result from the incorporation of that information into the mass of older information on presidential performance. Second, where Ostrom and Simon track twelve specific types of "presidentially relevant outcomes" (1985: 338) and associated expectational discrepancies, we have come to treat any piece of "results news" as the equal of any other. The evaluation of presidential performance represented by the Gallup "approval" level is a global judgment, and the ingredients of that judgment, we believe, are no less global. Our approach, among other things, makes fewer demands on the attention span of the citizen.

item since 1938 and has used the same sample design since 1949—continuities that make the Gallup time series very useful. As a general rule, the Gallup item in the hands of another survey organization (e.g., the CBS/New York *Times* Poll) produces trends that parallel Gallup and, in a given time period, finds levels of "approval" that are within sampling tolerances. Not surprisingly, variations in item wording or response options produce results that are harder to compare with the Gallup results.[14]

Our use of all available Gallup Poll information means that the time interval between any pair of polls is neither constant nor within our control. In recent presidencies Gallup has routinely polled more frequently than in past presidencies, and the frequency of polling increases with breaking news; in fluid situations, AIPO has polled as often as three times in a single month. In the second Truman presidency, AIPO averaged one poll every two months. The rate doubled with the Eisenhower presidency—in the average month between 1953 and 1960, AIPO carried out 1.12 surveys in which the "job handling" question was asked. The Johnson Administration and the Vietnam War were accompanied by a substantial increase in the frequency of polling; between 1963 and 1968 AIPO averaged 1.44 polls per month. President Nixon's first term and President Ford's term were polled at about the same pace as the Johnson presidency—with averages of 1.34 and 1.46 polls per month.[15] But breaking news can affect even this stepped-up pace: Nixon's Watergate term found AIPO in the field an average of 1.7 times per month. The Carter Administration was subject to even more polling than Nixon's Watergate term; between 1977 and 1980 the AIPO average was 1.94 per month.

14. For detailed comparisons of the various approaches to the measurement of support for the president, see Crespi 1980 and Orren 1978.

15. In the averages for the first Nixon term and the Ford presidency, I have corrected for AIPO's practice of not polling between June and November of the presidential election year. AIPO introduced the practice in 1972 and dropped it after 1980.

AIPO was only slightly less energetic during the first Reagan term, carrying out 79 surveys between 1981 and 1984, for an average of 1.65 polls per month.

The variation in the length of time between polls means that we have to choose between two alternatives in the handling of the dependent variable, each of which has consequences for the handling of independent variables. We can use all the polls, which has the virtue of preserving all of the information in the time series but necessitates correcting for variation in the interval between polls, or we can average the polls over some arbitrary time period—usually one month—to match the availability of time series performance data such as the CPI or unemployment statistics. The latter approach loses some information, especially in periods with fast-breaking events. In the research reported here, the full data set is used. The independent variables have been constructed in a way that reduces the effect of variability in the length of time between polls (the "poll period"). But since these procedures are not problem-free, they will be detailed, where necessary, in the discussion of particular operational measures.

Independent Variables. To account for public attention to an issue area, we look to both presidential prerogative and media practice.[16] The former, which represents the president's capacity to draw attention to a particular policy or problem area, is indexed by the number of presidentially generated television broadcasts in a given poll period divided by the length of the poll period. The measure, as employed by Haight, is content-

16. A detailed and technical account of operational procedures can be found in Timothy Haight's dissertation (1978: 157–89). Haight reviews the choice of measures and discusses the reliability of the measures we employ. Our close collaboration on the development of the thesis meant that its procedures reflect our common understanding of the best way to proceed. Since that time, because of our geographical separation, my thinking on these matters has developed without the opportunity for collaboration with Haight. In the analyses that follow, our joint understanding is reflected in the material on the Kennedy through Ford Administrations. Such new ideas as I have had will be examined in data on the Carter and Reagan Administrations.

free and stands as a test of the hypothesis that by calling attention to himself, the president can improve his "approval"
rating (Haight & Brody 1977). The effect of media practice on
the public's agenda is embedded in our procedures for story
selection and coding: the source of national news that has
the largest audience reach is network evening television news,
but complete and systematic archiving of these news programs
did not begin until 1968, and Vanderbilt University's *Television
News Abstracts and Index* was not published before 1972. This
means that before 1972 our recovery of the "most important
story of the day" (the single event given the greatest media attention) has to be from non-television sources. The most consistently available source from 1961 to 1972, and the one we
use to simulate network television news, is the New York
Times. From 1972 through 1980, we draw our daily story from
the CBS evening television news broadcast. In the New York
Times we select the front-page story in the right-most column
unless it is a local New York story, in which case we take the
front-page story in the left-most column. On television we
choose the lead story, i.e. the main story before the first commercial. We choose these stories because editorial practice signals that they are the most important news of the day, and because they are the stories that are most likely to come to the
attention of American citizens, to be remembered, and to enter
into the evaluation of the president (Iyengar & Kinder, 1987).[17]

17. Benjamin Page and I validated our assumption that before 1972 the
New York *Times* story we selected would also appear on evening news broadcasts (Brody & Page 1972: fn. 38). For the Johnson data set, the rate of agreement was 84 percent; for the Nixon data set, the rate of agreement was 86 percent. It seems unlikely that the restricted circulation of the New York *Times* is
a major source of error variance for stories as prominent as those we select as
the "most important story of the day." In a separate study, I selected a 100-day
random sample of the evening news broadcasts between 1972 and 1980; this
sample can be used to test the assumption that the three networks' story selection criteria are similar enough to permit using the highest-rated network
news broadcast (CBS) to represent all three networks. If we define "common
stories" as those that appear on the same evening on all three networks,
we find that between 56 and 60 percent of the network news is composed of

The selected stories are coded in accordance with the theory developed in the previous section. The codes distinguish foreign from domestic news, and in some administrations we create special categories to reflect intense news attention to particular issues—e.g. Vietnam, Watergate, and domestic economic news. These areas are further subdivided into news that originates within and outside the administration. Within these areas we distinguish news about policy proposals (which we sometimes refer to as "talk") from stories reporting results. "Results" stories are coded as "good," "bad," or "neutral" depending upon how they reflect upon presidentially set expectations. Coders are instructed to use policy "scripts" to judge how "results" news reflects upon the president.

Frequent experiments with the data have led to simplification of this complex coding scheme. We have found that issue-area distinctions and whether or not a story originates with the administration do not matter. Indeed, the greater density of news that results from collapsing across these distinctions yields more stable estimates. This result should not surprise; given the pace of polling and our use of but one story per day, as few as fourteen stories are used to create our news measure for many poll periods. Our coding scheme is too rich for such thin coverage, but practical and theoretical considerations preclude increasing our coverage; collapsing across categories is the ob-

---

common stories. This means that about 13 of the 22 minutes of the average evening's news are devoted to stories that appear on the three networks. The common stories are disproportionately likely to appear early in the broadcast—34 percent of the common stories appear in the first quarter of the CBS evening news (this 9 percentage point discrepancy is significant [$\chi^2 = 1439.16$]). In other words, the common stories are treated as important stories. This fact notwithstanding, the implicit assumption that the public is exposed to CBS's most important story on a given night irrespective of its viewing habits is far enough from the mark that the decision to choose CBS to reduce the volume of material to be coded carries with it the penalty of introducing measurement error. Unfortunately, the impracticality of coding twelve years—1972–84—of daily television news on more than one network requires that I pay this penalty.

vious alternative. The simplified coding scheme comes down to coding "talk" and "results" news, with the latter divided into "good," "bad," and "neutral."

"Results" news is combined to form the data for our principal independent variable, the "news ratio." The ratio is created for each poll period by subtracting the number of "bad" results stories from the number of "good" results stories and dividing by the total number of results stories. A given period's news ratio becomes part of the "cumulative news ratio," which is constructed, in accordance with Anderson's "averaging" model, as the sum of the "news ratios" up to and including the present poll period divided by the number of poll periods. In the analyses that follow, we will refer to this cumulative results ratio simply as the "news variable."

To test the hypothesis that "policy proposals" do not affect aggregate public opinion, we construct a "talk" variable that is the average number of proposal stories per poll-period day.

Finally, as the chapter on presidential honeymoons suggests, if we are going to focus on "approval" as a dependent variable, in presidential first terms we will have to distinguish the early months from the rest of the four years. Haight operationalizes this "early term" variable as the number of days since the president's inauguration subtracted from 180, divided by 180, and multiplied by six (Haight 1978: 189). The variable declines regularly from six to zero over the president's first six months in office. The day chosen as the entry into the formula is the midpoint of the poll period.

In the next two chapters I will investigate the model outlined in this chapter with data on Kennedy through Reagan's first term. Chapter Seven covers Kennedy through Ford; the Carter and Reagan presidencies will be examined in Chapter Eight.

CHAPTER 7

Daily News and Public Support for the President, Kennedy Through Ford

THE MODEL PRESENTED IN Chapter 6 hypothesizes, first, that the public in evaluating presidential performance responds to information on the attainment of policy goals, second, that public attention to a given issue area is primed by the quantity and quality of news coverage (Iyengar & Kinder 1987), third, that policy results—rather than policy proposals—will be the basic ingredient of the evaluation, and finally, that information on current policy results is combined with information on past results to determine the direction and amount of opinion change. The model asserts that the public uses easily available—media borne—information in form-

The data analyses reported in this chapter are the product of the collaboration between the author and Timothy Haight. Some of these results have been previously reported (Haight & Brody 1977; Haight 1978). Through a series of inadvertences and geographical moves by Dr. Haight, the content analyses—which are the heart of this chapter and which are for all practical purposes not reproducible—have been lost. This severely limits the analyses that can be undertaken with the presidencies Kennedy through Ford. It also precludes adding the data for the Carter and Reagan Administrations. Nevertheless, the analyses found in this chapter are sound. Further specification of the model will be undertaken in Chapter 8.

TABLE 7.1

Topic Areas of the Most Important Stories,
Kennedy Through Ford

Presidential term	Foreign policy	Domestic policy	N
Kennedy	76.8%	23.2%	1,000
Johnson[a]	68.7	31.3	1,752
Nixon I	57.6	42.4	1,212
Nixon II	32.9	67.1	496
Ford	35.6	64.4	483

SOURCE: Haight 1978, recomputed from Table 14.
NOTE: Vietnam stories are included in "Foreign policy" and Watergate stories are included in "Domestic policy."
[a]These figures cover the entire Johnson presidency.

ing and updating its impression of presidential performance. A test of this assertion begins with the examination of the major areas of news from 1961 to 1976. Table 7.1 presents the relative balance of domestic and foreign policy stories in this period.

As we can readily see, the amounts of attention the media paid to foreign and domestic policy news changed substantially over the period. The most prominent stories in President Nixon's second term were much more likely to be domestic than was the case in earlier presidencies. This marks a sharp break from the pattern of news in the Kennedy, Johnson, and first Nixon Administrations, when foreign policy dominated the news. Watergate is obviously involved in the change, but it is not simply a matter of Watergate. The shift in focus persisted through the Ford Administration, despite the continuation of the war in Vietnam into the second year of his term. After 1973, almost two-thirds of the most important stories concerned Watergate, the economy, and other domestic policy news.

If the hypotheses that guide this research are correct, the importance of foreign and domestic policy news in the public's assessment of the president's performance will differ before and after 1972. This may explain the change in the usefulness of measures of macroeconomic performance in helping us account for the dynamics of support for recent—post-Watergate—

presidents.[1] The public does not have to have changed its standards of judgment, but it may be more likely now than it was in the past to be primed to attend to indicators of macroeconomic success or failure. This emphasis on domestic policy may in turn reflect a shift in governmental (presidential) priorities as the Cold War with the Soviet Union has declined in centrality, the U.S. has withdrawn from the "hot" war in Vietnam and Cambodia, and security problems have lost their priority position on the agenda to domestic economic concerns.

This highlights a difference in the flexibility of models based on macroeconomic indicators and models based on broader measures of policy: the economy-based models do not prepare us to understand shifts in the relationship between support for the president and indicators of economic strength or weakness. Under the terms of these models the impact on presidential approval of a unit of inflation, unemployment, or real income should be constant irrespective of what else is going on in the world. Broader policy-based models lead us to expect that the impact of the economy on judgments of presidential performance will depend on its prominence in the mix of information available to the public.

Testing the assertions of the information processing model of opinion formation requires the further distinction between news that reports the outcome of policy and news that reports policy proposals. Table 7.2 separates news into "results" and "proposal" stories for the presidencies between 1961 and 1976. Considering both the foreign and domestic policy arenas, between 70 and 80 percent of the leading news stories in these presidencies report policy results as distinguished from proposals. There is a trend across the period: we can observe a small but steady decline in the appearance of proposal news over time. We will see a dramatic change in this trend when we examine the Carter and Reagan presidencies in the next chapter. However, for now we note that between 1961 and 1976 the

1. See the discussion of these shifts in Chapter 5.

136 Kennedy Through Ford

TABLE 7.2

Topic Areas of the Most Important "Results" and "Proposal" Stories, Kennedy Through Ford

Presidential term	Foreign policy		Domestic policy	
	"Results"	"Proposal"	"Results"	"Proposal"
Kennedy	56.3%	20.5%	13.3%	9.9%
Johnson[a]	46.9	21.8	22.9	8.3
Nixon I	40.4	17.2	29.8	12.6
Nixon II	25.4	7.5	53.4	13.7
Ford	29.6	6.0	51.3	13.0

SOURCE: Same as for Table 7.1.

NOTE: Vietnam stories are included in "Foreign policy" and Watergate stories in "Domestic policy." N is the same in each presidential term as in Table 7.1.

[a]These figures cover the entire Johnson presidency.

public had a large and increasing body of news about policy outcomes upon which to base its evaluations of Kennedy, Johnson, Nixon, and Ford.

In addition to the trend in the mix of results and proposals, Table 7.2 makes plain the alteration in the grounds for the public's evaluation of presidential job performance from the foreign to the domestic spheres. The performance of President Kennedy was about four times as likely to be judged on foreign policy outcomes as on the results of domestic policy. During President Johnson's years in office, despite the growing intensity of the war in Vietnam—which alone accounts for 22.5 percent of all results stories between 1963 and 1968—the ratio of foreign to domestic results stories was only half that of President Kennedy. President Nixon's first term saw a further reduction in this ratio: between 1969 and 1972 the most prominently featured news carried about one-and-one-third stories reporting a foreign policy result for every domestic result story presented. Not surprisingly, President Nixon's second term changed all this. With increasing emphasis on inflation and unemployment, the declining pace of the war in Vietnam, and the unfolding of the news about Watergate, the balance of results news shifted thoroughly to the domestic side. During Nixon's truncated second term, news reporting policy outcomes con-

tained two domestic stories for every foreign policy story—
Watergate "results" alone accounted for nearly a third (31.7 percent) of the 496 most prominent stories between January 1973
and August 1974. Domestic results were nearly as dominant
during President Ford's two and a half years in office as they
were during President Nixon's second term, but the type and
valence of news was quite different. The dominant themes during this period were the end of the war and the onset of both
inflation and recession—"stagflation"—as the most prominent domestic problem.

Distinguishing between news reporting policy results and
that reporting policy proposals is but the first step in trying to
understand the role of news in the dynamics of support for the
president. Within the set of stories reporting policy outcomes,
our model tells us that changes in support follow from changes
in the balance between stories that reflect favorably or unfavorably upon expected policy outcomes—expectations set either by societal consensus or presidential emphasis. Table 7.3
gives us a view of the aggregate balances among results stories
from 1961 through 1976, which vary considerably from presidency to presidency but in a general way accord with opinion
trends during the two decades. For the time being let us ignore
news of policy results that reflect neither positively nor nega-

TABLE 7.3

Distribution of Positive, Neutral, and Negative Results,
Kennedy Through Ford

Presidential term	Foreign policy			Domestic policy			N
	Pos.	Neut.	Neg.	Pos.	Neut.	Neg.	
Kennedy	18.7%	45.1%	17.1%	5.7%	8.2%	5.2%	696
Johnson[a]	18.4	22.6	26.1	8.9	15.9	8.1	1226
Nixon I	9.8	24.5	23.2	8.4	21.9	12.1	851
Nixon II	7.9	7.6	16.6	3.0	22.2	42.6	390
Ford	6.4	22.2	7.9	12.8	35.3	15.3	391

SOURCE: Same as for Table 7.1.
NOTE: Vietnam stories are included in "Foreign policy" and Watergate stories in "Domestic policy."
[a]These figures cover the entire Johnson presidency.

tively on presidential performance (the stories coded "neutral"). Leaving these neutral stories aside, President Kennedy's term presented the public with roughly equal proportions (52 : 48) of favorable and unfavorable policy outcomes. President Kennedy is the only one of the four presidents who enjoyed a positive news balance.

During the five years that President Johnson was in the White House, in foreign policy favorable news was outweighed by unfavorable news (41 : 59). Positive and negative domestic policy news were in about equal balance. But as we shall see, President Johnson's 1963–64 term was distinctly different from his 1965–68 term. In the year after the Kennedy assassination, with his successes in Congress prominently featured and the war in Vietnam largely invisible to the American people, Johnson enjoyed a substantial positive news balance. In the second Johnson term, with the intensification of the Vietnam War and our apparent failure to achieve our goals by military efforts, and with the growth of inflation, the positive news balance gave way to a surplus of negative news.

The first Nixon term continued the trend toward a strongly negative news balance. Between 1969 and 1972 the media carried only one story reporting favorable policy outcomes for every two reporting unfavorable outcomes (66 : 34). Not surprisingly, this imbalance was substantially magnified during President Nixon's second term. Watergate, problems with the economy, the OPEC shock, and other outcomes that reflected poorly on Nixon's performance made up 85 percent of the news reporting policy results between January 1973 and August 1974.

The negative imbalance was not nearly so pronounced during President Ford's term. On average, for every story reporting a positive policy outcome there were about 1.2 stories reporting a negative result. Against the background of the preceding term the Ford presidency must be seen as a substantial return to normality, yet we also see the continuing trends for the focus of the news to move from foreign policy to domestic policy and toward negative news balances. It is the latter trend that is im-

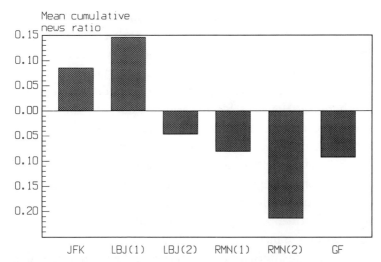

Figure 7.1. Cumulative News Ratio in the Average Poll Period, Kennedy Through Ford.

portant for the dynamics of public support, and we need to examine it a little more closely.

The distributions of results stories presented in Table 7.3 suggest the stimuli to which the public was exposed when judging presidential performance. The cumulative news ratio is a more dynamic version of this information. In Chapter 6 the "news ratio" [NR] for a given poll period was defined as the difference between positive [POS] and negative [NEG] results news expressed as a fraction of all results news [TOTAL RESULTS]—positive, negative, and neutral:

$$NR_t = (POS_t - NEG_t)/TOTAL_t.$$

The "cumulative news ratio" for a given period is the sum of the NR_ts, up to and including the current period, divided by the number of periods [t] through the current period. Figure 7.1 reports the cumulative news ratio in the average poll period in each of the presidential terms.[2] Figure 7.1 makes it quite clear that after the Kennedy presidency and the halcyon days of

2. In this analysis, President Johnson's term from 1963 through 1964 is considered separately.

President Johnson's political successes in the year before the 1964 election, the public, in an average period before a Gallup Poll, was presented with more and more news that reflected unfavorably on presidential performance. The Watergate period is, of course, substantially below the trend line; how could it be otherwise? However, leaving aside President Nixon's second term, we cannot fail to notice that between 1965 and 1976 the public was presented with more and more negative news with which to evaluate the performance of the president. By our construction of negative news, this means that increasingly over the period societally agreed-to goals were not being met or policy performance was increasingly falling short of expectations set by the incumbent president.

There is an alternative explanation to the trend observed in these data: we may well ask whether changes in media practice did not produce this trend. The data in Figure 7.1 also suggest that Vietnam, Watergate, and President Ford's pardon of his predecessor could have created a "crisis of confidence" in the presidency. In response to this alleged loss of confidence, the media may have soured on the presidency and increasingly accentuated the negative in reporting the news. Such a response on the part of journalists is a conceivable source of the increasingly unfavorable balance of results news over this period. Assessment of this hypothesis that press behavior and not the world of events has changed will have to await a detailed look within the Carter and Reagan presidencies in Chapter 8. But, based on analyses of the Carter and Reagan terms, I am not inclined to "blame the messenger." I find it difficult to sustain the contention that Vietnam, Watergate, and the Nixon pardon had so strained the credibility of the presidency for the press that evidence of successful presidential performance would be underplayed while evidence of policy failure was exaggerated.

If the trend toward negative news does not reflect a change in press behavior, what is its source? I am inclined to trace the increase to changing conditions in the world and an increase in

the scope of responsibilities of American government. Beyond
Vietnam and Watergate, the world faced by American leaders
has gotten much more difficult in two respects. In the first
place, American strategic military power has been revealed to
be primarily useful in a limited range of situations, namely to
deter Soviet aggression against Western Europe and the United
States. This is not a trivial achievement, but when deterrence
works it produces non-events and, in consequence, little in the
way of news. In rare nuclear crises—e.g. the Cuban missile crisis—deterrence gets full press attention, but the ordinary func-
tioning of our strategic deterrent does not fit the definition of
"news." On the other hand, the apparent failure of American
military might to achieve a victory in Vietnam, to deter ter-
rorism, or to affect the outcome of regional conflicts has given
rise to many reports of the "frustration of power."

The second respect in which the world has gotten more
difficult is a consequence of changes in the correlation of the
international economic system and the system of military
power. The world may be bipolar in military terms, but it is
multipolar in economic terms, and the United States no longer
enjoys the primacy it did in the two decades following World
War II.

To the president of the United States these changes mean a
much more complex set of problems with which to deal con-
structively. To the American people the revelations about the
limitations of American military power and the shift in our
relative economic position have meant a rising tide of news of
the "humiliation" of the United States by foreign terrorists and
by regional powers, of oil shocks, trade deficits, declines in the
dollar, international debts, and other signs of the loss of economic position. The press does not have to accentuate the
negative; the world does that well enough unaided.

Nor is the world outside the United States the only source
of bad news. The American people have asked their government to take responsibility for addressing a vast and growing

array of problems and in recent years have increasingly signaled an unwillingness to provide the resources for creating
public policy responses to the problems. This has led, among
other things, to press attention to both the continuation of the
problems and the inadequacy of the government's response.
Whether these trends are ineluctable remains to be seen. However, over the period that has been the focus of this chapter
there was an accelerating negative balance to news of policy
results.

A consequence of the shifts in the political system—both
internationally and domestically—is that changes in the mix
of foreign and domestic news have not produced radical changes
in the balances of negative and positive news. From 1965 to
1976, irrespective of which policy area was most prominent,
bad news has outweighed good news and the imbalance has
grown.

The question remains whether the news helps us understand the dynamics of support for the president. Our approach
to the question is to estimate a multivariate statistical model
of the Gallup approval and disapproval ratings in the presidential terms between 1961 and 1976. In addition to the news
variable, the statistical model includes (1) an "early term" variable, reflecting the expectation that approval will be different
during the "honeymoon" months, and (2) a measure of presidentially generated television, to examine whether, apart from
the news, a president can use his access to the media to affect
his standing with the public. Table 7.4 presents the results of
Haight's exploration of this question (1978: 213). In general, all
three variables relate to the production of disapproval of presidential job handling; approval responds to the news and to TV
appearances. These analyses indicate that any observed differences in approval in the early months and the rest of the term is
due to a difference in the mix of the news and/or to a positive
public response to presidentially generated television.

The cumulative news measure does far and away the best

TABLE 7.4
Explaining Public Approval of the President,
1961–76

Explanatory measure		Dependent variable	
		Percent approving	Percent disapproving
Cumulative news	β	90.98	−96.63
	(t)	(17.23)*	(19.10)*
TV appearances	β	25.59	−25.00
	(t)	(2.90)*	(8.77)*
Early term	β	0.15	−1.20
	(t)	(0.40)	(3.20)*
Constant	α	57.08	29.21
Statistics:	R²	.64	.71
	F	137.45	191.94
	P_F	.00	.00
	N	241	241
	DW	.48	.54

SOURCE: Haight 1978: Table 23.
*$P_t \leq .05$.

job of helping us understand the ebb and flow of support for the president. The public coordinates changes in its evaluation of the president with incremental changes in the mix of "results" news. If the news in a given period indicates that consensus policy goals are not being met, and/or that policy outcomes that the president has led the public to expect have failed to materialize, the next Gallup Poll is likely to find a decrease in public approval and a corresponding increase in disapproval.

In the "early term" or "honeymoon" period, approval of presidential performance is unusually high because of the favorable mix of news to which the public is exposed and to a lesser extent because of the greater volume of presidentially generated television early in the term (Haight 1978: 265ff). In other words, as far as public approval is concerned, there is no reason to consider the early days special. This is not the case with respect to disapproval: in the first few months of a president's first term, considering other factors, disapproval is unexpectedly low. Taken together the two equations indicate that this unusually low level of disapproval is not converted into higher levels of approval but rather translates into a reluctance to express either approval or disapproval.

Presidential discretionary television is an independent and statistically significant explanatory factor during this period. Presidents appear to be able to augment the positive effect of good policy outcomes and to limit the damage from bad policy news by speaking directly to the American people. However, the president's capacity to use television is limited. A comparison of the coefficients for the news variable and the TV appearance variable indicates that a president is unlikely to be able to call enough press conferences or give enough television speeches to more than marginally mitigate the impact of a sustained run of "bad" news. Moreover, as experienced political figures presidents appear to recognize this limitation and are not anxious to meet the press when the news is bad. Haight's data indicate that presidents are more likely to independently generate television when the news is good than they are when the news is bad (*ibid.*: 264).[3]

Table 7.4 brings to light a technical problem that urges caution in our interpretation of the results. The Durbin Watson (DW) statistic for these presidencies shows autoregression in the residuals. Ideally the DW statistic should fall into the range $1 \leq DW \leq 2$ if we are to have full faith in the precision of the estimates.

A Brief Stocktaking

The data analysis for the period 1961–76 supports the general outline of the theory of public opinion developed in Chapter 6. In the aggregate, public approval of the way the president is

3. The rank-order correlation between the cumulative news ratio in the average period (Figure 7.1) and the average number of TV appearances per day (Haight 1978: 264) across these presidential terms is $r_s = 1.0$. Even for so limited a number of cases, this is impressive.

handling the job stems from the accumulation of media-borne impressions that the president is succeeding in achieving the policy goals set by societal consensus or by his own policy proposals. The mix of policy areas in which goal attainment will be judged will vary from president to president. The ingredients of the mix will reflect both the president's own newsworthy efforts and newsworthy problems brought to the fore by forces over which the president has little or no control. However, the source of an outcome appears not to matter to the public; what matters is how the reported outcomes reflect upon goal attainment.

These preliminary explorations of the impact of news on public support for Presidents Kennedy, Johnson, Nixon, and Ford set the stage for more intensive investigations of the Carter and Reagan presidencies. Chapter 8 reports these investigations.

Daily News and Public Support for Presidents Carter and Reagan

THE CARTER PRESIDENCY AND the Reagan first term offer an opportunity to extend our analyses and to bring other factors to bear in exploring the sources of public support for the president. These two presidential terms are especially interesting because they present patterns of public support that are different from each other and, in the case of President Reagan's first term, different from those we have previously examined. Figure 8.1 presents the approval pattern for the two presidencies. There are several notable features in this figure. The most unexpected one is the striking similarity in the patterns of public support during each president's first two years in office. All the talk about President Reagan's supposed immunity to negative news—the "teflon president," the "Great Communicator," and the like—and Carter's alleged lack of attractiveness to the American people is apparently without foundation. Based upon the public's general response to their performance, there is no reason to treat President Carter and President Reagan as special cases.

Reagan started with less initial support than Carter, proba-

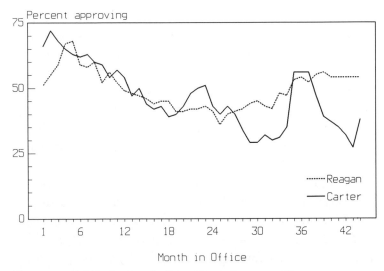

Figure 8.1. Public Approval of Presidents Carter and Reagan.

bly a consequence of the distribution of partisanship in the American electorate (see Chapter 2 above). The assassination attempt at the end of March 1981 erased this initial deficit; in the wake of the shooting, Reagan's level of approval rose to a point at which he received positive ratings from about two-thirds of the American people. This put him even with President Carter at the same point in his presidency. Over the next 23 months of their respective terms both Carter and Reagan lost about a third of their early support. But then—about 25 months into their presidencies—the trends diverge. Beginning early in 1983—perhaps as a consequence of the continued decline in inflation and the waning of the 1982–83 recession—President Reagan's support recovered. At the time he stood for reelection, he was evaluated positively by six Americans in ten.

The rallies following the Camp David summit and the Iran hostage crisis are clearly visible in the data on the public response to President Carter's handling of the presidency. The Camp David accords were doubly positive for Carter. The summit became the center of attention, and the absence of hard

news gave the opposition no basis for criticism of foreign policy while the talks were in progress. After the accords were
reached, President Carter enjoyed an unusual volume of news
reporting positive policy outcomes. The Iran hostage crisis is
a rally event pure and simple. Support for President Carter
cycled with elite criticism (see Chapter 3 above). Unlike Camp
David, there was no news of positive results to add to the increase in support fueled by the elite's suspension of criticism of
Carter's foreign policy.

At 25 months—the point at which President Reagan's support began its recovery—President Carter's approval rating re-
sumed its slide after the rally associated with the Camp David
accords had run its course. His support leveled off at about
30 percent and remained there until the rally occasioned by the
Iranian hostage crisis carried his level of approval back above
50 percent. This rally boost dissipated in the spring of 1980. Beyond this point—perhaps as a result of the worsening state
of the economy and frustration over the lack of success in getting the hostages released—President Carter's support quickly
dropped to its pre-crisis level.

Our findings about the sources of public support for Presidents Kennedy, Johnson, Nixon, and Ford in the last chapter
suggest that we look to news of policy outcomes in our attempt
to explain the Carter and Reagan trends displayed in Figure 8.1.
We will begin our examination of the most important news
stories in the Carter and Reagan administrations by comparing
them with news during the presidential terms examined in
Chapter 7.

Daily News in the Carter and Reagan Presidencies

Analyses of public opinion in the Kennedy, Johnson, Nixon,
and Ford presidencies indicate that the distinction between foreign and domestic news is without consequence for the dy-

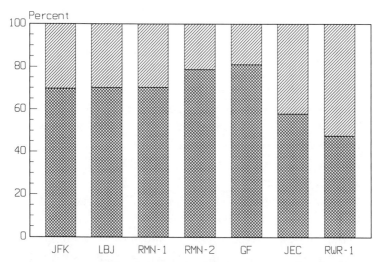

Figure 8.2. News of Policy Results (Dark Cross-Hatching) and Proposals (Light Cross-Hatching), Kennedy Through Reagan 1.

namics of presidential support; the American people apparently react in much the same way to news originating at home and abroad. However, the public distinguishes between and responds differently to reports of policy outcomes and policy proposals. In the aggregate, public opinion[1] appears to be unaffected by news of policy proposals. By contrast, there is a definite link between news of policy outcomes and aggregate evaluations of presidential performance. Figure 8.2 presents the distributions of results and proposal news in the most important news stories during the Carter and Reagan presidencies. For comparison the same distributions are presented for the presidencies of Kennedy, Johnson, Nixon, and Ford.

With respect to the balance of these two types of news, the Carter and Reagan terms are clearly different from previous ones: in the Kennedy and Johnson presidencies and in President Nixon's first term, 70 percent of the leading news stories reported policy outcomes or some other form of results news;

1. More properly, the opinion of the marginal opinion holder.

in Nixon's second term and the Ford presidency eight leading news stories in ten report results. But stories reporting results appear much less frequently during the Carter and Reagan years. Fewer than six stories in ten between 1977 and 1980 and less than half of the most important stories during President Reagan's first term report policy outcomes or other results that reflect on presidential performance. The public had substantially less information about policy results to use in forming its impressions and evaluations of Carter and Reagan than it did in earlier presidencies.

The greater volume of reports of policy proposals during the Carter and Reagan terms alerts us to the possibility that this kind of news played a different role in the dynamics of support for President Carter and President Reagan than it did for Presidents Kennedy, Johnson, Nixon, and Ford. Before exploring this possibility we need to examine the evaluative content of daily news in the Carter and Reagan terms.

In Figure 8.3, news from the periods of the Carter and Reagan presidencies is added to our comparison of the distributions of positive, neutral, and negative results reported during

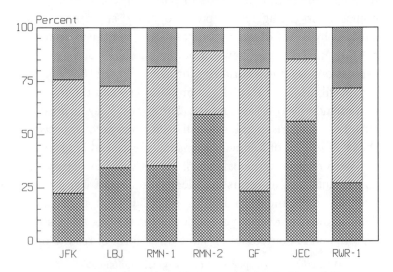

Figure 8.3. Distributions of Results News, Kennedy Through Reagan 1 (top, positive; middle, neutral; bottom, negative).

the Kennedy, Johnson, Nixon, and Ford presidencies. Clearly, the public received a large proportion of negative results news during the Carter presidency. More than half (56 percent) of the results stories from 1977 through 1980 were classified as negative. This means that, from the perspective of a consensus on desirable results or expectations that President Carter had set, Americans were getting a lot of bad news. The Carter figure is exceeded only during President Nixon's Watergate term— where 59 percent of the stories were classified as negative. The proportion of negative news in President Carter's term is half again larger than that for the Johnson presidency and President Nixon's first term, when just over a third of the stories were classified as negative. A lot of Carter's "bad news" resulted from coverage of the embassy takeover in Teheran and the ensuing hostage crisis. In the early months of the crisis this bad news did not reduce support for President Carter, but the rally came to an end with the reemergence of elite criticism of the handling of the hostage crisis. In 1980, both Iran and the state of the economy made substantial contributions to the generation of negative news by which the Carter performance was judged.

By a small margin President Reagan's first term shows the largest proportion of positive results news among the seven presidencies presented in Figure 8.3.[2] For every item of negative news reported between 1981 and 1984 an item of positive news appeared. Only the Kennedy presidency matches this one-to-one ratio. The Johnson and Ford terms are not far behind the Kennedy and Reagan terms, with a ratio of negative to positive stories of 5 : 4. The Nixon and Carter presidencies show large surpluses of negative results. During the Carter term the public saw or read about four negative stories for each positive story. The ratio in the Nixon presidency is 2 : 1 negative in the first term and nearly 6 : 1 negative during the Watergate term.

The notion of a "cumulative news ratio" [CNR] was intro-

---

2. Positive stories were 28.6 percent of the results news between 1981 and 1984; they were 27.3 percent during the Johnson years.

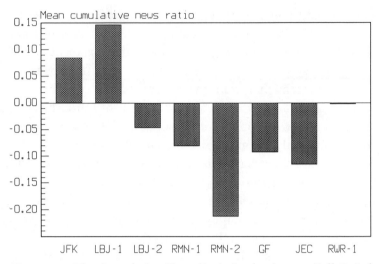

Figure 8.4. The Cumulative News Ratio in the Average Poll Period, Kennedy through Reagan 1.

duced in Chapter 6 and used in Chapter 7 to help account for public support for Presidents Kennedy, Johnson, Nixon, and Ford. In Figure 7.1 we saw that after 1964 the CNR in the average poll period was increasingly negative. In Figure 8.4 we expand this analysis with the addition of data from the Carter and Reagan presidencies. The trend in the acceleration of negative CNRs, begun after 1964, continued through the Carter Administration. In Chapter 7, two possible sources of this trend were considered. In the first place, it was argued, more and more "bad" news could result from an increasingly harsh political reality both at home and abroad. For example, more intergovernmental conflict, stemming from the divided party control of the White House and Congress, or a failure of policy to ameliorate social and economic problems at home, might mean that policy outcomes would increasingly fall short of expectations. Outside the United States the international system is judged to be less cooperative and hospitable to the interests of the United States. These sorts of changes could give rise to a growing stock of negative news stories. In other words, under this hypothesis, there is more bad news reported because there is more bad news produced by changes in the political system.

Alternatively, changes in press practice resulting from the cynicism and loss of presidential credibility produced by Vietnam and Watergate could generate an acceleration of bad news. Under a change in press practice, for example, negative news would be sought out for its own sake or to satisfy reporters' and editors' need to portray politics in dark colors. Or negative stories of lesser news value might get more attention than similar stories would have gotten in previous presidencies. Given our criteria for story selection, such a change would give rise to more negative news being coded.

These are alternative but not necessarily mutually incompatible explanations of the increase in negative CNR's after 1964. Considering news aggregated over Carter's entire term, neither of these explanations is inconsistent with the data from his presidency. However, since the trend ended with the Carter presidency, neither helps us correctly anticipate the average cumulative news ratio for President Reagan's first term. Given the fundamental equality of positive and negative news in the average polling period in the Reagan first term, it cannot be the case that the world is inexorably producing more and more bad news. Nor can it be the case that Vietnam and Watergate produced a permanent change in press practice that made negative news more attractive. The simplest explanation for the pattern of average CNRs between 1961 and 1980 may be the best: When there is bad news it is reported; when there is good news it is reported. The pattern observed before the Reagan presidency is caused by a growing stock of manifestly bad news. Of course, some would argue, with Representative Patricia Schroeder, that the bad news was there in Reagan's first term but was ignored by the press. As we shall see this argument also proves false.

An examination of the average CNRs, disaggregated by year, during the Carter and Reagan presidencies gives us an-

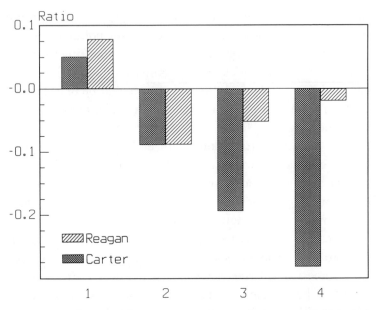

Figure 8.5. The Cumulative News Ratio in the Average Poll Period, Year by Year, in the Carter and First Reagan Presidencies.

other look at the plausibility of the several interpretations of the patterns of aggregate CNRs in Figure 8.4. These averages are displayed in Figure 8.5. The news ratio in the average poll period got progressively more negative in each year of the Carter presidency. But over the first year of his term, the CNR was positive. If reporters and editors were inappropriately seeking negative news in service of their cynicism, they were not successful in their search. A more plausible account is that what was going on was reported and that there was for Carter, as for previous presidents, more news favorable to his administration early in its first term (Grossman & Kumar 1981). During the Carter presidency's first year the news is more positive than one would expect under the hypothesis that the acceleration of bad news is a natural consequence of changes in the domestic and international political systems.

In the average poll period after Carter's first year, the public

TABLE 8.1

Cumulative News Ratio in the Average Poll Period,
Carter Presidency, Year by Year

Year	Mean	Variance	N	t-test	P_t
1977	0.050	0.0078	25	–	–
1978	−0.089	0.0007	24	7.38	≤ .005
1979	−0.194	0.0008	25	13.41	≤ .005
1980	−0.282	0.0001	16	11.70	≤ .005

NOTE: N = the number of poll periods; t-tests are for the means between adjacent years.

TABLE 8.2

Cumulative News Ratio in the Average Poll Period,
First Reagan Presidency, Year by Year

Year	Mean	Variance	N	t-test	P_t
1981	0.078	0.0030	19	–	–
1982	−0.088	0.0007	19	7.04	≤ .005
1983	−0.052	0.0068	22	1.78	≤ .05
1984	−0.019	0.0003	18	1.63	≤ .10

NOTE: N = the number of poll periods; t-tests are for the means between adjacent years.

was presented with an ever more negative CNR. The apparent acceleration of negative news is not illusory. The statistical tests reported in Table 8.1 indicate that the mean CNRs were significantly more negative each year between 1977 and 1980.

The annual news balances during the first term of the Reagan presidency, depicted in Figure 8.5, also make it hard to accept the notion that changes in the domestic and international political systems and/or in press practice inevitably give the American people an increasingly bleak picture of presidential performance. The information the public received in 1982 was much more negative than in 1981, but in 1983 the trend was reversed and the CNRs were less negative in 1983 and 1984 than in 1982. Table 8.2 presents tests of the differences in annual average CNRs during President Reagan's first term: the shift in the news balance from 1981 to 1982 and from 1982 to 1983 meet standard criteria of statistical significance;

TABLE 8.3

*Year by Year Differences in Cumulative News
Ratios in the Average Poll Period for the Carter and
First Reagan Presidencies*

Year in term	Δ_M	t-test	P_t
1	−0.028	1.19	≥ .10
2	−0.001	0.12	≥ .10
3	−0.142	7.77	≤ .005
4	−0.263	51.75	≤ .005

NOTE: Δ_M = mean for Carter minus mean for Reagan.

the decrease in the negative ratio from 1983 to 1984 is a bit less statistically reliable ($P_t \leq .10$), but it is probable that the apparent change is not illusory.

Table 8.3 reports the results of a statistical comparison of the annual average CNRs for the Carter and first Reagan presidencies. These tests indicate that during President Carter's and President Reagan's first two years in office the patterns of good and bad news were statistically indistinguishable. But the annual average CNRs were profoundly different from each other during the second half of their terms. As far as news of policy results is concerned, those who argue that the press treated Reagan differently from Carter may find support for their hypothesis in the data from the third and fourth years of their presidencies, but they will surely have difficulty accounting for the data in the first two years. It may be better instead to simply acknowledge that the press more or less reports the world it finds; differences in the patterns of press reports in the second half of the two presidential terms reflect differences in real world results.

These findings suggest that if public opinion responds to press reports of policy outcomes, the response is to real world politics and policy and not a manipulated image of that world. We turn now to an examination of the extent to which public opinion during these two terms responded to press reports of policy outcomes.

Sources of Public Support for Presidents Carter and Reagan

The analyses presented in Chapter 7 treat the reports of policy success or failure brought to the public by the media as the primary factor explaining support for the president. This approach is based on a simplifying assumption—namely, that public opinion responds to economic policy and outcomes in other policy domains to the extent they receive press attention.[3] In the following analyses this assumption will be relaxed for indications of economic performance. This will allow us to see whether unemployment and inflation affect public approval of presidential job handling directly or only to the degree they are attended to by the press.

Moving beyond media reports in developing an explanation of presidential support requires the introduction of additional variables and a phased approach. We expect news reports to be related to the evaluation of presidential performance. We also expect news reports to depend upon actual events and upon the sorts of coverage rhythms that Grossman and Kumar (1981) have identified. In order to better specify the effects of policy outcomes, we will begin with an analysis of sources of the CNR. The variables we will employ in this analysis are seven.

- □ Early Term. This is a dummy variable that takes on the value "1" during the first 180 days of the first term of an administration and is "0" thereafter. For reasons detailed in Grossman & Kumar 1981 and Chapter 2 above, we expect the news to be more positive during the early term period.
- □ Policy Proposals. This measure is the proportion of leading news stories that do not report political or policy outcomes. We do not have a theoretically derived expectation about the direction of link between the quantity of

3. Unfortunately, because of the unavailability of data, this assumption cannot be examined in the Kennedy to Ford presidencies.

proposal news and the Cumulative News Ratio.[4] However, non-results news was such a large part of the coverage from 1977 to 1984 that we are curious about its role in support for Presidents Carter and Reagan. For technical reasons, in order to satisfy our curiosity about an impact on public opinion, we must include the measure in the first stage of the analysis as well.

□ Inflation. This is a measure of the annualized rate of change in the Consumer Price Index. An increase in inflation is expected to produce negative news.

□ Unemployment. This is a measure of the current rate of civilian unemployment. As with inflation, we expect an increase in unemployment to produce negative news.

□ Lagged Approval. This variable, which is the percent approving of presidential job performance in the previous period [Approval$_{(t-1)}$], is expected for two reasons to relate positively to the Cumulative News Ratio in the current period. Good poll numbers in themselves are often occasions for positive news stories. Additionally, they also appear to increase the likelihood of presidential success, which in turn generates "good news."

□ Iran Crisis. This is a dummy variable that has a value of "1" between November 4, 1979, and May 4, 1980, and a value of "0" during the rest of the Carter presidency. This variable is included here to insure correct specification in the second phase of the analysis. We expect that the CNR during the hostage crisis will be negative.

□ Lagged Cumulative News Ratio. In order to obtain proper estimates of the effects of various types of substantive indicators on the Cumulative News Ratio, we need to include the CNR for the previous time period—$(t-1)$—in our analysis.

Table 8.4 reports the analyses using these variables to explore the sources of the Cumulative News Ratio in the two presidencies. In only one respect are the results for the Carter presidency different from those for President Reagan's first term. News of policy proposals is positively related to the CNR during President Carter's term. In the average poll period be-

4. We will use two-tailed tests of significance in cases such as this where no direction of effect is specified.

TABLE 8.4

Sources of Cumulative News During the
Carter and Reagan Presidencies

(*Generalized least squares estimation*)

Variable	Measure	Carter	Reagan
Early Term	β	0.03	0.03
	(t)	(1.98)*	(3.68)*
Policy Proposals	β	0.0006	−0.00004
	(t)	(4.04)*	(0.33)
Inflation	β	−0.0005	−0.00004
	(t)	(0.49)	(0.06)
Unemployment	β	−0.007	−0.003
	(t)	(1.09)	(0.77)
Approval$_{(t-1)}$	β	0.0005	0.0008
	(t)	(1.00)	(1.07)
Iran Crisis	β	−0.01	n/a
	(t)	(0.69)	n/a
CNR$_{(t-1)}$	β	0.85	0.74
	(t)	(14.50)*	(11.95)*
Constant	α	−0.02	−0.02
	(t)	(0.56)	(0.34)
Statistics:	R^2	.95	.94
	N	89	77
	Rho^a	.046	.006

NOTE: Values followed by an asterisk (*) are significant at the level of $P_t \leq .05$, one-tailed probability.
^{a}Values of Rho $\geq$ .30 indicate that significant auto-correlation remains.

tween 1977 and 1980, 42 percent of the most important daily news stories reported policy proposals rather than results; at this level the CNR would be positively incremented about two-and-a-half percentage points.

Because it is unique to the Carter presidency, no ready explanation of the finding suggests itself. It may be happenstance. It is reminiscent of Rivers's findings about the relationship of popularity and support for presidential proposals in Congress (Rivers & Rose 1985). Clearly proposal news is more easily manipulated by a president than is news of policy outcomes. But if policy successes encourage presidents to submit proposals—a reverse in causal direction with the CNR affecting the rate of the introduction of proposals—why have other presidents not seized this opportunity?

The CNR was positively incremented during the honeymoon period of both the Carter and Reagan presidencies. During the first six months of both presidential terms it was three percentage points more positive than we would otherwise expect. Clearly, the strongest component of the CNR in any given poll period is inertia. We are, after all, dealing with a "cumulative" measure that combines past and present; we would not expect it to change abruptly. Since substantive stories do not inherently occur in long time series, it is not surprising that the inertial component is dominant.

Unexpectedly, the statistical indicators of inflation and unemployment were not systematically related to the CNR. One's memories of the Carter and Reagan presidencies include the recollection that one or another aspect of the economy figured prominently in the news. The analytic necessity of including the lagged CNR may mask the relationship of inflation and unemployment to the news. For the Carter presidency, both inflation and unemployment are more important with the inertial component of news removed.[5] Similarly, for Reagan unemployment may be more important than Table 8.4 indicates.[6] However, memories are a weak reed upon which to build an analysis and the estimates in Table 8.4 are the best basis upon which to proceed.

There is another way to look at the link of the economy to the news. The expectation that the news will reflect economic performance is partly confounded, during these two presidential terms, by the complex interrelationships among inflation, un-

5. With the lagged CNR omitted, the GLS coefficients for inflation ($\beta = -0.003$) and unemployment ($\beta = -0.026$) have t-ratios with associated one-tailed probabilities approaching significance ($P_t \leq .10$). However, the Rho coefficient for the equation (Rho = .58) indicates that auto-correlation remains. Moreover, since the time-series for these economic indicators also includes a strong inertial component, we cannot be certain that inflation and unemployment are not simply imperfectly substituting for the lagged CNR.

6. With "lagged CNR" omitted, the coefficient for unemployment ($\beta = -0.02$) has a significant negative impact on the CNR between 1981 and 1984 (t-ratio = 2.18; $P_t \leq .05$). However, auto-correlation remains a problem (Rho = .70) and the caveats expressed in the previous footnote apply here as well.

employment, and the CNR.[7] The correlations are sizable and, in some instances, a bit strange. Some of the "strangeness" results from the negative relationships between inflation and unemployment. A decrease in one source of economic woe tends to increase the other source of woe. This creates a policy problem—namely, how to stimulate growth without producing inflation—and it can also affect coverage. We expect that inflation will produce negative news, and it does in Carter's term; however, it is associated with positive news during Reagan's first term. We also expect that unemployment will be negative news. It is during Reagan's term, but it is correlated with positive news during Carter's presidency.

These perverse relationships may have their source in several factors. First, we need to consider an administration's policy emphases in relation to the president's core economic constituency. Republicans are more inflation-averse than are Democrats, and Democrats are more unemployment-averse than are Republicans (Hibbs 1982). Second, we need to look at performance expectations in the policy area that is *not* emphasized by the president. And third, we have to assess media attention to the lack of goal attainment with respect to the de-emphasized area. This assumes that a president has only limited power to shift press attention—and consequently public attention—away from the unaddressed problem. This could also indicate that the media emphasizes and the public responds to "negative" rather than "positive" results (Bloom & Price 1975). However, both the press and the public responded positively to the decline in unemployment and inflation in 1983 and 1984.

7. The following matrix of zero-order coefficients describes the associations of the three variables in the two presidencies. Coefficients in the upper triangle are for the Carter presidency; those in the lower are for the Reagan presidency.

	CNR	Inflation	Unemployment
CNR		−.48	.22
Inflation	.51		−.35
Unemployment	−.74	−.39	

A switch in focus to the "unsolved" problem is not evidence of a preference for negative results.

For Carter and Reagan there is a clear switch to the unsolved problem. President Carter came into office committed to fighting recession and unemployment. The negative relationship between inflation and unemployment meant that to the extent unemployment came down, inflation tended to rise. The CNR reflects this fact, and the decline in unemployment appears to be perversely related to the CNR. The same phenomenon affected President Reagan—until unemployment turned around in 1983—with inflation and unemployment exchanging places.

At the second stage of the analysis we move to an investigation of the sources of support for Presidents Carter and Reagan. Table 8.5 details the results of this investigation. The structure of support for President Carter is quite different from that for President Reagan. Apart from the rally period of the Iran hostage crisis and the massive effect of inertia in public approval, President Carter's support ratings are wholly dependent upon indications of policy success or failure brought to public attention by news reports. If we consider Tables 8.4 and 8.5 together, we see that for President Carter even his "honeymoon" depends upon the unusually high Cumulative News Ratios during the first six months in office. The Reagan "honeymoon" relates to positive news in about the same degree as the Carter "honeymoon," but, in addition to the indirect effect of news during the early part of the term, President Reagan's approval ratings during these early months are about two percentage points higher than we would otherwise expect.

In general, the impact of news on President Reagan's support is much weaker than on President Carter's support. Other things being equal, in the average poll period—with CNR = −0.115—President Carter's approval rating would be down three percentage points from the previous period simply on the basis of news reports of policy outcomes. By contrast, in the

TABLE 8.5

*Sources of Support During the Carter and
Reagan Presidencies*

(*Generalized least squares estimation*)

Variable	Measure	Carter	Reagan
Cumulative News	β	26.58	16.42
	(t)	(3.45)*	(1.73)*
Early Term	β	−0.25	2.35
	(t)	(0.12)	(1.78)*
Policy Proposals	β	−0.02	0.05
	(t)	(1.06)	(1.59)
Inflation	β	−0.12	−0.18
	(t)	(0.86)	(1.91)*
Unemployment	β	1.15	−3.18
	(t)	(1.43)	(5.76)*
Approval$_{(t-1)}$	β	0.69	0.32
	(t)	(11.26)*	(3.06)*
Iran Crisis	β	8.02	n/a
	(t)	(4.24)*	n/a
Constant	α	11.55	61.58
	(t)	(2.16)*	(6.54)*
Statistics:	R^2	.91	.91
	N	89	77
	Rho^a	−.074	.018

NOTE: Values followed by an asterisk (*) are significant at the level of $P_t \le$ .05, one-tailed probability.
^{a}Values of Rho $\ge$ .30 indicate that significant auto-correlation remains.

average Reagan poll period—with CNR = −0.021—public approval would be .003 percentage points below the figure for the previous period. Looked at differently, in the average poll period, other things being equal, the impact of news on evaluations of President Carter is about a thousand times greater than its impact on evaluations of President Reagan.

The impact of news is clearly present in President Reagan's first term but diminished to a degree by the direct effect on his approval ratings of other indicators of policy success and failure. Neither inflation nor unemployment directly affects support for President Carter, but they are important ingredients of the public's evaluation of President Reagan. With inflation at its average level for Reagan's first term (about 5 percent), the approval of his performance in office is about one-and-a-half percentage points lower than at minimum inflation for the term. Unemployment was substantially more important; at its average for the first term (about 8.7 percent), President Reagan's approval is about five percentage points lower than with unemployment at its minimum for the term (about 7 percent).

Before leaving Table 8.5 we should take note of "policy proposals." It was argued in Chapter 6 that because of the role played by the political elite in opinion formation and because of the opportunities for partisan position-taking on policy proposals, news of such proposals should be subject to a deep partisan discount. Haight demonstrates that this is the case for the presidencies of Kennedy, Johnson, Nixon, and Ford (1978). Since non-results stories are a large fraction of the news during the Carter and Reagan presidencies, we were led to wonder whether their popularity might be more sensitive to this type of news than was the case with Kennedy, Johnson, Nixon, and Ford. Table 8.5 shows that the larger volume of proposal news between 1977 and 1984 seems not to have made any difference. Carter and Reagan, like previous presidents, were evaluated on the basis of policy outcomes.

Summing Up

The investigation of media and public opinion during the Carter and Reagan presidencies, added to the findings in Chapter 7, can be used to refine our appreciation of the sources of support for the president.

Public evaluations of presidential performance have a very large inertial component. This means that, on the basis of our data, the public is not as fickle and "moody" as it is sometimes portrayed (see, for example, the accounts in Almond 1950 and Rosenau 1961). The public can and does rapidly revise its evaluation of presidential performance; these large shifts almost always take place in the wake of unanticipated international events—crises—that catch the elite unprepared as well. Most of the time international crises add to presidential support but, given enough negative criticism by legitimate commentators, a president can also suffer a substantial loss in approval (Brody & Shapiro 1989). However, rally gains and losses are episodic. Their effects pass and inertia is reestablished.

The inertia in the system does not preclude changes in levels of support; it means that levels will change gradually. Our data indicate that, by and large, change in public opinion is a response to impressions of presidential success and failure formed from indications of policy outcomes reported in the news. News reports prime the public to attend to areas of public policy (Iyengar & Kinder 1987) and also provide the basis for the public's evaluative response.

The public can also respond to unmediated indicators of presidential policy performance. The direct influence of indicators of macroeconomic performance on support for President Reagan shows that the public does not exclusively rely on the media. Unfortunately, these data do not speak to the circumstances that give rise to unmediated instead of mediated effects of policy outcomes.

The fact that the macroeconomy was relatively volatile and newsworthy in both the Carter and Reagan presidencies makes more puzzling the differences in the role played by macroeconomic indicators in the dynamics of support for these two presidents. For President Carter the economy and all other influences on public support have their impact through the media. For President Reagan press reports influence support, but inflation and unemployment also affect the public's evaluation of his job performance independently of the macroeconomy's effects on the news. Looking back over the two presidential terms, we find no obvious cause for these differences in the structure of public support.

There is an additional difference in the structure of the dynamics of support for Carter and Reagan. President Carter's high level of support during the first seven months he was in office is indirectly a product of the positive news reported during those early months. In this respect, President Carter's support is structured no differently from that of previous presidents.[8] President Reagan's approval ratings were about two percentage points higher than we would otherwise expect in the first seven months he was in office. This may be a result of the public's reaction to the assassination attempt and/or to the successful policy dynamism of the Reagan Administration above and beyond the public's reaction to the positive news produced by these events.

The intriguing differences in nuance aside, the fundamental picture of the interactions of the president, policy, the press, and the public that emerges from these analyses is quite clear. Over the quarter century from the Kennedy inaugural to the Reagan reelection, the American people have evaluated the performance of their president on the evidence of policy success and failure supplied to it by the press. The standards of "success" and "failure" are derived from outcomes for which there is general agreement—prosperity is "good," war is "bad," and so forth—and from the expectations set by the president and his administration—"if we are allowed to do this, this good thing will result." In the aggregate, the public seems to respond to policy outcomes, not the means of achieving them—it is pragmatic rather than ideological.

Policy proposals as such appear to be heavily discounted. This and the phenomenon of the rally response are products of the dependence of the public on opinion leadership in situations of uncertainty. Proposals give rise to uncertainty because they usually generate debate—often fairly technical debate—among political elites about how a public policy problem is to be solved. In any given policy area few Americans are confident

8. In Table 7.4 we saw that the "early term" variable is not significantly related to approval. However, the analyses in this chapter (Table 8.4) suggest that this results from the direct effect of the honeymoon on news during these early months; the CNR is more positive during the early months of the term, and that is the means by which the honeymoon affects popularity.

that they know the best or even an effective solution. In such a situation, members of the public, if they are moved to form an opinion at all, tend to respond to opinion leaders in whom they otherwise have confidence. Under this account, the division in the elite will condition the impact of a given proposal on changes in public opinion. A balanced division is unlikely to give rise to a net shift in opinion; an unbalanced division is likely to mean a decisive acceptance or rejection of the proposal and, accordingly, provide a political result to which the public can respond.

What are we to make of a public like this one? What do our findings tell us about the principal questions underlying most research on public opinion—namely the "quality" of the democratic citizen and the possibility of democratic control of public policy? These are the questions to which we will turn in the final chapter.

CHAPTER 9

Public Support for the President and Democratic Control of Public Policy

FROM THE ANALYSES IN the preceding chapters we can draw a composite picture of the factors that influence an average American citizen's evaluation of the performance of the incumbent president:

Americans ordinarily do not pay close attention to the actions of their government, but this lack of attention does not preclude the formation of impressions of how government in general, and the president in particular, are handling their jobs. These impressions at any point in time are compounded of an inertial component and new information.[1] While there are

---

1. For an excellent discussion of the cognitive foundations of "impression-driven" models of political evaluations, see Lodge, McGraw & Stroh 1989. The central points they make can be summarized as follows. First, impression formation is "on-line," that is, judgments are made as relevant information is encountered. Second, the judgments are stored in memory as summary evaluations of the attitude objects—metaphorically, an "evaluation counter" or "judgment tally." Third, it is the summary evaluation that is revised in light of new information relevant to the judgment. And fourth, "when asked to voice an opinion, people typically retrieve their [current] summary evaluation from memory" (ibid.: 401). At this level of specificity there is no difference between the Lodge, McGraw & Stroh model and the information averaging model described in Chapter 6 and employed in this study.

circumstances under which rapid changes in the distribution of public support can be anticipated, the presence of inertia means that opinions will usually be fairly stable. Both the inertial component of public support and the new information that updates impressions of presidential performance are based on news reports of policy outcomes. These news reports do double duty: they focus public attention on areas of public policy in which performance is judged (Iyengar & Kinder 1987) and they also provide the main basis for the public's evaluative response. As noted in Chapter 8, the public can also respond to unmediated indicators of presidential policy performance. For example, the direct influence of indicators of macroeconomic performance on support for President Reagan shows that the public does not exclusively rely on the media. Unfortunately, as noted earlier, our data do not speak to the circumstances that give rise to unmediated rather than mediated effects of policy outcomes.

It is news of outcomes rather than reported policy announcements or proposals that ordinarily drives the process of opinion formation. The differential impacts of proposals and outcomes stem from the differences in the typical reaction of opinion leadership in the two situations. Proposals routinely give rise to partisan or ideological "position taking" by opposition elites (Mayhew 1974); in consequence, they are likely to be discounted on grounds of source credibility. In the presidencies examined in his study, policy proposals have been found to be unrelated to the dynamics of support.

Policy outcomes give rise to a more one-sided response on the part of the elite. Outcomes meeting the expectations set by the president give him and his partisans among the elite an opportunity to take credit; those which do not meet his expectations put the president on the defensive and give the opposition an opportunity to point to presidential shortcomings.

Even the exceptional circumstances of international crises demonstrate the importance of opinion leadership. When opposition elites avoid criticizing foreign policy failures, the public appears to ignore manifestly bad outcomes and increases its support for the president. International crises in which the opposition elite performs its usual role of criticizing presidential policy-making fail to produce rallies. And on the rare occasions when presidential partisans join in criticizing the president—as was the case during the early weeks of the Iran-Contra affair—an anti-rally can occur (Brody & Shapiro 1989).

By reporting changes in the status quo the press focuses public attention on this or that area of public policy. Opinion leadership conditions the response of the public to the news—the news that comprises the dynamic ingredient of support for the president. In the aggregate, the public seems to respond to policy outcomes rather than the means of achieving them; it is more pragmatic about results than ideological about means. How does this kind of "public" meet the concerns of democratic theorists? Can the "public" we find in this study satisfy the requirements for democratic influence in the policy process?

The obvious way for the public to influence public policy is by being an "electorate," which is to say, by choosing policy-makers. The public's judgment of presidential performance is electorally relevant. The standard of evaluation of incumbent performance—successful policy-problem solving—translates into electoral behavior that constrains a policymaker to "be successful." This appears to be a rather weak constraint, but upon reflection it offers some prospects for democratic control.

The role of performance evaluation in the vote decision increases the size and heterogeneity of the constituency the president *should* have in mind when considering policy. In principle, the entire media-exposed public becomes the president's "reelection" constituency.[2] In its turn, a shift in con-

2. See Fenno 1978: 1–30, for distinctions among "constituencies." The "reelection" constituency is composed of those who generally support the candidate; in the case of the president, these would be his supporters from the previous election, whom the incumbent would wish to have vote for him or his party in the next election. Fenno creates these distinctions for the constituencies of members of Congress who are not, as is the president, limited in the number of terms they can serve. The fact that a president can only serve two

stituency can affect the attractiveness of policy alternatives. To the extent presidents are interested in retaining their or their political party's hold on the presidency they will be less inclined to choose policy alternatives simply on the basis of the ideology or interests of their "primary" constituency; satisfying the reelection constituency's desire for policy outcomes will be important as well. Unless an alternative favored by the primary constituency has as high a probability of yielding success as the most potentially successful alternative, it will be less attractive to an incumbent motivated by reelection. A shift in the relative weights of pragmatic and ideological considerations in policy-making is no small matter.

The public's pragmatism does not necessarily preclude policy innovation, not even risky innovations. This seems a contradiction, since "risk" and "success" are to some degree at odds with each other. The contradiction is reduced by the partial capacity of a president to focus media attention and by the roles that the media play in determining the areas in which performance will be judged. If risky innovations are not accompanied by massive publicity, they are less likely to come to public attention and affect the public's evaluation of presidential performance. If they are announced by the president with great fanfare and they fail, presidential support will decline. President Carter's attempts at welfare reform in the spring of 1977 offer us an example (Lynn & Whitman 1981). Risky innovations undertaken without publicity that fail to achieve their goals[3] cannot always be kept from the public—the 1985–86 Iran "arms for hostages" swap is a massive example of this truth. After all, both failure and its being publicized are part of the risk. But even a cautious president need not be frozen into

---

terms could lead to an "uncontrolled" president in the second term. However, the effects of evaluation of the incumbent on the electoral fate of the candidate of the incumbent president's party (Brody & Sigelman 1983) should ensure against "last-period" effects (Ferejohn 1986: 9–10).

    3. One assumes that innovations that succeed will be well publicized.

inaction by a fear of failure and the ensuing loss in public support. The inertia in public opinion means that the effects of any given failure—unless it is as completely misbegotten as was the Iran-Contra affair—will not be great.

Manipulation of the press by the president would tend to reduce public influence in the process of policy-making. Presidents certainly attempt to get a favorable press, and some are better at it than others.[4] A president's capacity to control news—and thereby shape public opinion—is circumscribed by the constitutionally independent centers of power in the courts and, especially, in Congress and by the institution of a free press. The system may favor the president (Gans 1979), but there is ample opportunity for others to address the American people.

The pragmatism of the public and the inertia in public support that have emerged in this study also tend to defend the public against manipulation. The fact that impressions are cumulative tends to reduce the impact of policies whose timing is chosen with regard to the electoral cycle (Tufte 1978; Nordhaus 1975). If opposition political leaders choose to speak out, the public will not have its attention diverted from poor performance by foreign policy crises, summits, and the like. The centrality of "results" in the public's judgment of the president means that a flurry of policy pronouncements will not rescue a president's support from a surplus of bad news.

Institutional and opinion formation processes that help protect the American public from manipulation also keep it a part of the policy process. In the language of the economic theory of institutions, these processes offer the American people

4. Hertsgaard 1988 gives a fulsome description of the efforts of the Reagan White House to control the news. If his account is accurate, Reagan was more successful than other presidents in putting a favorable spin on the news. But "more success" is a difference in degree. All presidents, since FDR showed the way, make the attempt. But the press is not without resources either (Grossman & Kumar 1981).

(the "principal") some measure of control over the president (its "agent").[5] In a recent paper John Ferejohn has essayed the conditions that permit collective principals (like electorates and publics) at reasonable cost to keep agents (like the president) accountable. Our study speaks directly to two of Ferejohn's conditions: "[if] the principal [is] able to commit to a schedule of rewards and punishments that depends on the outcomes of the agent's actions, a very high degree of control is achievable" (Ferejohn 1990: 6).

As we have seen, increasing, maintaining, and withdrawing support for the president—which represents the public's capacity for reward and punishment between elections—is almost entirely based on outcomes. The fact that outcomes that affect public opinion do not necessarily depend on the president's actions may weaken the degree of control, but there is more than enough link between presidential action and public reaction to ensure that a prudent president will take the public response to outcomes into account in considering alternative policy options.

Ferejohn points out that elected officials are not without resources in attempting to wrest control from their "principals." If they can establish competition among voters for particularistic policy rewards, officials can "exploit the electorate completely" (*ibid.*: 8). However, "[i]f electors [or members of the public] could somehow bind themselves not to listen to blandishments of officials seeking to play one group off against another . . . officials would be unable to exploit divisions among them" (*ibid.*: 9). The findings in this study suggest that the public is relatively immune to "blandishments." Policy proposals do not appear to contribute to support.

The question of "exploitable divisions" in the public is a more complex matter and one that deserves an extended treat-

5. For brief but illuminating discussions of the application of the principal/agent model to the problem of political control, see Ferejohn 1986 and 1990.

ment. Such an extended treatment would be out of place here, but we have something to say on the matter. The research reported here has focused almost exclusively on the sources of change in aggregate public opinion because it is this dynamic that is relevant to presidential politics. But questions of the sources of public support among the partisan subgroups within the public have been looked into (Haight & Brody 1977; Haight 1978). From these studies and from the investigation of partisan subgroups in "rally" situations, it is apparent that sometimes the evaluations of the president across the partisan subgroups move in concert and sometimes they do not.

The factors that appear to distinguish occasions in which the partisan subgroups react in concert from those in which they do not are the clarity or ambiguity of results that are relevant to evaluation and the length of time in which a particular story dominates the news. The clearer the results and the more news devoted to a particular topic, the less likely it is that reactions will differ along lines of partisanship. During the Vietnam War period in the Johnson presidency and the Watergate period in President Nixon's second term, the opinions of members of the partisan subgroups moved along the same track; this is also true of the periods of economic recession in the Eisenhower and Reagan presidencies. By contrast, ambiguous results and a more varied menu of topics apparently give partisanship an opportunity to affect opinion formation. During the first Nixon term and the Kennedy presidency, the partisan subgroups show substantially different patterns of evaluation of presidential performance.

The determinants of a partisan response to news would appear to be outside the capability of a president to control—Johnson could not prevent Democrats from deprecating his performance during Vietnam nor could Nixon maintain his base of support among Republicans as Watergate came to light. In other words, there are circumstances in which there are partisan divisions in the public, but these are not necessarily exploitable.[6]

The key to the "problem of agency" is basing rewards and punishments on performance and resisting particularistic blandishments that allow agents to exploit divisions. The American people—despite minimal attention to politics, despite a lack of information, and because of the peculiar institutions of American politics—appear to have stumbled upon the key.

Over the past two hundred years—even over the twenty-five years covered in this study—the responsibilities of the American president have expanded. The evolution of the presidency means that more recent presidents will be judged on success or failure in areas that their predecessors boldly stepped into for the first time and that became part of the routine expectations of the office. Presidents are also judged in policy areas in which they innovate. The areas in which presidential performance is judged are by no means exclusively domestic. The expansion of the role of the United States in the international system after the Second World War, the growing complexity of the system as alliances are strained, the increased dependence of the United States on strategic materials that we do not control, and the emergence of new governments and dozens of para-governmental terrorist organizations have brought forward problems that the president cannot ignore. Depending upon the emphasis given to these areas by the president, the elite, and the media, policy on any of these problems can become the focus of public attention and be judged according to its evident success or failure.

In more than a rhetorical sense, the president is always on trial before the American people but the jury is almost always out. New evidence is delivered each day and that evidence is

6. The public is of course divided along numerous other lines. To my knowledge, no one has investigated whether any of these cleavages are related to responses to the news.

weighed with the accumulation of evidence from the past. On the basis of the new and past evidence a tentative verdict is reached. Occasionally the jury is polled and these polls have a political life of their own. The final verdict is not delivered until election day, but every day during the four years before election day the public has been having its attention drawn to presidential performance and has been drawing conclusions from what it sees and reads. There is rough justice and a source of public influence in this process. A very long way from "all power to the people," but democracy nonetheless.

References Cited

References Cited

Abelson, R. 1976. "Script Processing in Attitude Formation and Decision Making." In J. S. Carroll and J. W. Payne, eds., *Cognition and Social Behavior*. Hillsdale, N.J.: Earlbaum.

Achen, C. 1975. "Mass Attitudes and the Survey Response," *American Political Science Review*, 69: 1218–37.

Adams, W. 1984. "Recent Fables about Ronald Reagan," *Public Opinion*, 7, no. 5: 6–9.

AIPO [American Institute of Public Opinion]. 1975. "Campaign '76," *The Gallup Opinion Index, Report No. 125* (Princeton, N.J.). Nov.–Dec.

Almond, G. A. 1950. *The American People and Foreign Policy*. New York: Harcourt, Brace & Co.

Anderson, N. H. 1974. "Cognitive Algebra: Integration Theory Applied to Social Attribution." In L. Berkowitz, ed., *Advances in Experimental Social Psychology* (vol. 7, pp. 1–101). New York: Academic Press.

Axelrod, R. 1978. "Communication: 1976 Update," *American Political Science Review*, 72: 622–24.

Bagdikian, B. H. 1983. *The Media Monopoly*, Boston: Beacon Press.

Behr, R. L., and S. Iyengar. 1982. "Television News, Real World Cues, and Changes in the Public Agenda." Paper presented at the 37th annual meeting of the American Association of Public Opinion Research, Hunt Valley, Md.

Bloom, H. S., and H. D. Price. 1975. "Voter Response to Short-Run Economic Conditions: The Asymmetric Effect of Prosperity and Recession," *American Political Science Review*, 69: 1240–53.

Bogart, L. 1981. *Press and Public: Who Reads What, When and Why in American Newspapers*. Hillsdale, N.J.: Earlbaum.

Bond, J. R., and R. Fleisher. 1982. "Presidential Popularity and Congressional Voting: A Re-Examination of Public Opinion as a Source of Influence in Congress." Paper delivered at the annual meeting of the American Political Science Association, Denver, Colorado, Sept. 2–5.

Braestrup, P. 1978. *The Big Story*. Garden City, N.Y.: Anchor Books.

Brody, R. A. 1982. "Public Evaluations and Expectations and the Future of the Presidency." In J. S. Young, ed., *Problems and Prospects of Presidential Leadership in the Nineteen-Eighties*, vol. I. Washington, D.C.: University Press of America. Pp. 37–56.

Brody, R. A., and B. I. Page. 1972. "The Impact of Events on Presidential Popularity: The Johnson and Nixon Administrations." Paper presented at the annual meeting of the American Political Science Association, Washington, D.C.

———. 1973. "Indifference, Alienation and Rational Decision." *Public Choice*, 15: 1–17.

———. 1975. "The Impact of Events on Presidential Popularity: The Johnson and Nixon Administrations." In A. Wildavsky, ed., *Perspectives on the Presidency*. Boston: Little, Brown.

Brody, R. A., and C. R. Shapiro. 1989. "Policy Failure and Public Support: The Iran-Contra Affair and Public Assessments of President Reagan," *Political Behavior*, 11.

Brody, R. A., and L. Sigelman. 1983. "Presidential Popularity and Presidential Elections: An Update and Extension," *Public Opinion Quarterly*, 47: 325–28.

Brody, R. A., and P. Sniderman. 1977. "From Life Space to Polling Place," *British Journal of Political Science*, 7: 337–60.

Case, J. 1981. *Understanding Inflation*. New York: Penguin Books.

Converse, P. E. 1975. "Public Opinion and Voting Behavior." In F. I. Greenstein and N. W. Polsby, eds., *Handbook of Political Science*, vol. 4. Reading, Mass.: Addison-Wesley. Pp. 75–169.

Crespi, I. 1980. "The Case of Presidential Popularity." In A. H. Cantril, ed., *Polling on the Issues*. Cabin John, Md.: Seven Locks Press.

Dahl, R. A. 1961. *Who Governs?* New Haven, Conn.: Yale University Press.

Edwards, G. C., III. 1980. *Presidential Influence in Congress.* San Francisco: W. H. Freeman.

Erbring, L., E. N. Goldenberg, and A. H. Miller. 1980. "Front Page News and Real World Cues," *American Journal of Political Science,* 24: 16–49.

Feldman, S. 1982. "Economic Self-Interest and Political Behavior," *American Journal of Political Science,* 26: 446–66.

Fenno, R. 1978. *Home Style.* Boston: Little, Brown.

Ferejohn, J. A. 1986. "Incumbent Performance and Electoral Control," *Public Choice,* 50: 5–25.

———. 1990. "Information and the Electoral Process." In J. A. Ferejohn and J. H. Kuklinski, eds., *Information and Democratic Processes.* Urbana: University of Illinois Press. Pp. 1–19.

Fiorina, M. P. 1978. "Economic Retrospective Voting in American National Elections," *American Journal of Political Science,* 22: 426–43.

Gans, H. 1979. *Deciding What's News.* New York: Pantheon.

Greenstein, F. 1965. *Children and Politics.* New Haven, Conn.: Yale University Press.

———. 1982. *The Hidden-Hand Presidency: Eisenhower as Leader.* New York: Basic Books.

Grossman, M., and M. Kumar. 1981. *Portraying the President.* Baltimore, Md.: The Johns Hopkins University Press.

Haight, T. 1978. "The Mass Media and Presidential Popularity." Ph.D. dissertation, Department of Communication, Stanford University, Stanford, Calif.

Haight, T., and R. A. Brody. 1977. "The Mass Media and Presidential Popularity," *Communication Research,* 4: 41–60.

Hertsgaard, M. 1988. *On Bended Knee.* New York: Farrar, Straus, & Giroux.

Hibbs, D. A., Jr. 1972. "Problems of Statistical Estimation and Causal Inference in Dynamic, Time-Series Regression Models." Paper delivered at the annual meeting of the American Political Science Association, Washington, D.C.

———. 1979. "The Mass Public and Macro-Economic Performance: The Dynamics of Public Opinion towards Unemployment and Inflation," *American Journal of Political Science,* 23: 705–31.

———. 1982. "The Dynamics of Political Support for American Presidents among Occupational and Partisan Groups," *American Journal of Political Science*, 26: 312–32.

———. 1987. *The American Political Economy*. Cambridge, Mass.: Harvard University Press.

Iyengar, S., and D. R. Kinder. 1987. *News that Matters*. Chicago: University of Chicago Press.

Iyengar, S., D. R. Kinder, and M. D. Peters. 1982. "Priming Effects in Politics." Mimeo, Yale University, March.

Iyengar, S., M. D. Peters, and D. R. Kinder. 1982. "Experimental Demonstrations of the 'Not-So-Minimal' Consequences of Television News Programs," *American Political Science Review*, 76: 848–58.

Janowitz, M. 1968. "Communications, Mass." In *International Encyclopedia of the Social Sciences*, vol. 3. New York: Macmillan, Free Press. Pp. 41–55.

Katz, D., and P. Lazarsfeld. 1955. *Personal Influence: The Part Played by People in the Flow of Mass Communications*. Glencoe, Ill.: Free Press.

Keene, K. 1980. "Rally 'Round the President," *Public Opinion*, 3, no. 2: 28–29.

Kelley, S., and T. Mirer. 1974. "The Simple Act of Voting," *American Political Science Review*, 68: 572–91.

Kernell, S. H. 1975. "Presidential Popularity and Electoral Preference. A Model of Short-Term Political Change." Ph.D. dissertation, University of California, Berkeley.

———. 1978. "Explaining Presidential Popularity," *American Political Science Review*, 72: 506–22.

———. 1986. *Going Public: New Strategies of Presidential Leadership*. Washington, D.C.: CQ Press.

Kiewiet, D. R. 1983. *Macroeconomics and Micropolitics*. Chicago: University of Chicago Press.

Kinder, D. R. 1981. "Presidents, Prosperity and Public Opinion," *Public Opinion Quarterly*, 45: 1–21.

Kinder, D. R., and D. R. Kiewiet. 1979. "Economic Discontent and Political Behavior," *American Journal of Political Science*, 23: 495–527.

———. 1981. "Sociotropic Politics," *British Journal of Political Science*, 11: 129–61.

Kinder, D. R., and W. R. Mebane, Jr. 1982. "Politics and Economics in Everyday Life." In K. Monroe, ed., *The Political Process and Economic Change*. New York: Agathon.

Kinder, D. R., G. S. Adams, and P. W. Gronke. 1989. "Economics and Politics in the 1984 Presidential Election." *American Journal of Political Science*, 33: 491–515.

Kinder, D. R., S. Iyengar, J. A. Krosnick, and M. D. Peters. 1983. "More than Meets the Eye: The Impact of Television News on Evaluations of Presidential Performance." Paper presented at the annual meeting of the Midwest Political Science Association, Chicago.

Kline, E. 1984. *Gender Politics*. Cambridge, Mass.: Harvard University Press.

Kramer, G. H. 1971. "Short-Term Fluctuations in U.S. Voting Behavior, 1894–1964," *American Political Science Review*, 65: 131–43.

———. 1983. "The Ecological Fallacy Revisited," *American Political Science Review*, 77: 92–111.

———. 1984. "Reply to Scicchitano," *American Political Science Review*, 78: 791–92.

Ladd, E. C., Jr. 1979. "The Candidates and the State of the Presidency," *Fortune* (3 Dec.): 38–44.

Lane, R. 1962. *Political Ideology*. New York: Free Press.

Lee, J. R. 1977. "Rallying 'Round the Flag: Foreign Policy Events and Presidential Popularity," *Presidential Studies Quarterly*, 7: 252–56.

Lodge, M., K. M. McGraw, and P. Stroh. 1989. "An Impression-Driven Model of Candidate Evaluations." *American Political Science Review*, 83: 399–419.

Lynn, L. E., Jr. and D. deF. Whitman. 1981. *The President as Policy Maker*. Philadelphia: Temple University Press.

MacKuen, M. 1981. "Social Communication and the Mass Policy Agenda." In M. MacKuen and S. Coombs, eds., *More Than News*. Beverly Hills, Calif.: Sage Publications.

Mayhew, D. R. 1974. *Congress: The Electoral Connection*. New Haven, Conn.: Yale University Press.

McGuire, W. 1968. "The Nature of Attitudes and Attitude Change." In G. Lindzey and E. Aronson, eds., *Handbook of Social Psychology*, vol. 3. Reading, Mass.: Addison-Wesley.

Monroe, K. R. 1979. "Econometric Analyses of Electoral Behavior: A Critical Review," *Political Behavior*, 1: 137–73.

———. 1984. *Presidential Popularity and the Economy*. New York: Praeger.

Mueller, J. E. 1973. *War, Presidents and Public Opinion*. New York: John Wiley.

Neuman, W. R. 1976. "Patterns of Recall among Television News Viewers," *Public Opinion Quarterly*, 40: 115–23.

Neustadt, R. E. 1980. *Presidential Power: The Politics of Leadership.* New York: John Wiley.

——. 1982. "Presidential Leadership: The Clerk Against the Preacher." In J. S. Young, ed., *Problems and Prospects of Presidential Leadership in the Nineteen-Eighties*, vol. I. Washington, D.C.: University Press of America. Pp. 1–36.

Nie, N. H., and K. Anderson. 1974. "Mass Belief Systems Revisited: Political Change and Attitude Structure," *Journal of Politics*, 36: 540–91.

Nie, N. H., and J. N. Rabjohn. 1979. "Revisiting Mass Belief Systems Revisited," *American Journal of Political Science*, 23: 139–75.

Nisbett, R., and L. Ross. 1980. *Human Inference: Strategies and Short-comings of Social Judgment.* Englewood Cliffs, N.J.: Prentice-Hall.

Nordhaus, W. 1975. "The Political Business Cycle," *The Review of Economic Studies*, 42: 169–90.

Orren, G. 1978. "Presidential Popularity Ratings: Another View," *Public Opinion*, 1, no. 2: 35.

Ostrom, C. W., and D. M. Simon. 1985. "Promise and Performance: A Dynamic Model of Presidential Popularity," *American Political Science Review*, 79: 334–58.

Page, B. I., R. Y. Shapiro, and G. R. Dempsey. 1986. "What Moves Public Opinion." Mimeo, March.

Paldam, M. 1981. "A Preliminary Survey of the Theories and Findings on Vote and Popularity Functions," *European Journal of Political Research*, 9: 181–99.

Peffley, M., and J. T. Williams. 1985. "Attributing Presidential Responsibility for National Economic Problems," *American Politics Quarterly*, 13: 393–425.

Polsby, N. 1964. *Congress and the Presidency.* Englewood Cliffs, N.J.: Prentice-Hall.

Popkin, S., J. W. Gorman, C. Phillips, and J. A. Smith. 1976. "Comment: What Have You Done For Me Lately?," *American Political Science Review*, 70: 779–813.

Presser, S., and J. N. Converse. 1976–77. "On Stimson's Interpretations of Declines in Presidential Popularity," *Public Opinion Quarterly*, 40: 538–41.

Reid, T. R., and D. Broder. 1979. "Kennedy Attack on Shah Brings Critical Barrage," Washington *Post*, Nov. 22: A-21.

Rivers, H. D., and N. L. Rose. 1985. "Passing the President's Program: Public Opinion and Presidential Influence in Congress," *American Journal of Political Science,* 29: 183–96.

Rosenau, J. N. 1961. *Public Opinion and Foreign Policy.* New York: Random House.

Schattschneider, E. E. 1960. *The Semi-Sovereign People.* New York: Holt, Rinehart and Winston.

Schlesinger, A., Jr. 1973. *The Imperial Presidency.* Boston: Houghton Mifflin.

Schlozman, K. L., and S. Verba. 1979. *Injury to Insult: Unemployment, Class, and Political Response.* Cambridge, Mass.: Harvard University Press.

Scicchitano, M. J. 1984. "Comment on Kramer," *American Political Science Review,* 78: 790–91.

Shanks, M., M. Denney, S. Hendricks, and R. A. Brody. 1982. "Trade Off Reasoning. . . ." Paper presented at the annual meeting of American Political Science Association, Denver, Colorado.

Sigelman, L. 1979. "Presidential Popularity and Presidential Elections," *Public Opinion Quarterly,* 43: 532–34.

Sigelman, L., and P. J. Conover. 1981. "The Dynamics of Presidential Support During International Conflict Situations." *Political Behavior,* 3: 303–18.

Sniderman, P. M., and R. A. Brody. 1977. "Coping: The Ethic of Self-Reliance," *American Journal of Political Science,* 21: 501–21.

Sniderman, P. M., J. Kuklinski, and R. A. Brody. 1984. "Policy Reasoning and Political Values: The Problem of Racial Equality," *American Journal of Political Science,* 28: 75–94.

Stimson, J. A. 1976. "Public Support for American Presidents: A Cyclical Model," *Public Opinion Quarterly,* 40: 1–21.

Stokes, D. E. 1966. "Spatial Models of Party Competition." In A. Campbell, P. Converse, W. Miller, and D. Stokes, *Elections and the Political Order.* New York: John Wiley. Pp. 161–79.

Stone, P., and R. A. Brody. 1970. "Modeling Opinion Responsiveness to Daily News," *Social Science Information,* 9: 95–122.

Sullivan, J. L., J. E. Pierson, and G. E. Marcus. 1978. "Ideological Constraint in the Mass Public," *American Journal of Political Science,* 22: 233–49.

Tufte, E. R. 1975. "Determinants of the Outcome of Midterm Congressional Elections," *American Political Science Review,* 69: 812–26.

————. 1978. *Political Control of the Economy*. Princeton, N.J.: Princeton University Press.

Waltz, K. 1967. "Electoral Punishment and Foreign Policy Crises," in J. N. Rosenau, ed., *Domestic Sources of Foreign Policy*. New York: Free Press.

Weatherford, M. S. 1978. "Economic Conditions and Electoral Outcome: Class Differences in the Political Response to Recession," *American Journal of Political Science*, 22: 917–38.

Index

Index

In this index an "f" after a number indicates a separate reference on the next page, and an "ff" indicates separate references on the next two pages. A continuous discussion over two or more pages is indicated by a span of page numbers, e.g., "57–59." *Passim* is used for a cluster of references in close but not continuous sequence. Subentries are listed in page number order rather than alphabetical order.

ABC (network), 72, 110n

Activism, and popularity over time, 87–88

Adams, W., 105n

Alsop, Joseph, 77

American Institute of Public Opinion (AIPO), 127–29. *See also* Gallup Polls

Americans for Democratic Action, 67

Anderson, Norman, 126, 132

Approval ratings, 16n–23 *passim*, 99n; of Bush, 10–11, 35, 37, 39; of Carter, 10–14, 19, 35–39 *passim*, 58, 70f, 99, 101f, 146–48, 159–66 *passim*; of Reagan, 10–15 *passim*, 19, 27f, 32–37 *passim*, 43–44, 58, 73–75, 102, 103n, 146–47, 159–66 *passim*; of Ford, 19, 34, 37, 39, 58, 61, 103n; of Kennedy, 19, 34, 37, 39, 57, 99, 101f; in honeymoon period, 32–44 *passim*; and rally phenomenon, 56–74 *passim*, 87, 89; and economic performance, 99–103; information integration model and, 127–32 *passim*, 142–48 *passim*, 159–63 *passim*

Attention, public, 106–13 *passim*, 116, 127, 129–30, 133f, 161, 168f

Bacon, Francis, 122f
Bagdikian, Ben, 122, 123–24
"Baseline" policy area, public attention to, 113
Bay of Pigs incident (1961), 48–49, 68–70
Begin, M., 13
Behr, R. L., 112
Berlin crisis, 49, 62
Blame, attribution of, 105n
Blue-collar workers, and economic performance, 92–93
Bond, J. R., 21–22
Bowles, Chester, 69
Brody, R. A., 47f, 54–55, 107, 126
Bush, George, 7–11 *passim*, 35–39 *passim*

Calhoun, John C., 17
Cambodia, 61ff, 135
Camp David summit meeting, 13f, 147f
Capehart, Homer, 69
Carter, Jimmy, 10–15 *passim*, 22–23; approval ratings of, 10–14, 19, 35–39 *passim*, 58, 70f, 99, 101f, 146–48, 159–66 *passim*; AIPO polls and, 11–12, 20n; honeymoon period of, 12–13, 35–42 *passim*, 160–66 *passim*; and rally phenomenon, 13–14, 45, 56n, 58, 62, 70–77 *passim*, 147–48, 151; popularity of, over time, 88f; economic performance and, 95, 99–105n,

151, 162f, 165; attribution of blame to, 105n; information integration model and, 135, 140, 146–67; innovation by, 171
Castro, Fidel, 68f
CBS (network), 55, 72, 75, 110n, 131n
CBS/New York *Times* Poll, 16n, 55, 128
China, 7, 8–9
Chronic problems variable, in presidential popularity, 51–52
CIA, 69f
"Clerkship" responsibilities, of president, 115–16
"Coalition-of-minorities" variable, in presidential popularity, 50–51, 86–87
Cognitive psychology, 122–25
Cold War, 135
Comprehension, public opinion and, 106–7
Congress, 21–22, 23, 29, 65, 74, 159, 170n, 172
Connally, John, 72
Conover, P. J., 46, 71n
Converse, J. N., 86n, 117
CPS/NES survey, 12n
Crises, and the rally phenomenon, 22, 40–78 *passim*, 164–65, 169–70. *See also* War
Cuba, 48–49, 68–70, 141
Cumulative News Ratio (CNR), 132, 139–43 *passim*, 151–66n *passim*

Dahl, Robert, 22
Democracy: in Latin America, 7f; public opinion in, 17–18, 168–76

Democrats, 41–43, 67–76 *passim*, 92–95, 99–105n *passim*, 161

Depression (1930s), 108

Deterrence, military, 141

Diplomatic developments, and rally phenomenon, 49

Domestic policy: crises, 47–48; information integration model and, 134–37 *passim*, 148–49. *See also* Economy variables

Dominican Republic, 33, 41n, 49, 62f

Durbin Watson (DW) statistic, 144

"Early term" variable, 132, 142f, 157, 166n. *See also* Honeymoon period

Eastern Europe, 7, 8–9, 39

"Economic slump" variable, in presidential popularity, 50

Economy variables, 50, 51–52, 91–108 *passim*, 124; evaluation of, 105, 107–8, 162–65 *passim*, 169; and information integration model, 135, 141, 151, 157–65 *passim*; international, 141; partisan subgroups and, 174. *See also* Inflation; Unemployment

Editorial practice, and public attention, 109–12

Educational level: and opinion leadership, 55–56; and Stimson's model, 86n

Edwards, G. C., III, 21

Eisenhower, Dwight D.: honeymoon of, 32–39 *passim*; and rally phenomenon, 57, 62, 67–71 *passim*, 76; popularity

of over time, 83, 87f, 104; economic performance and, 102–3, 174; and AIPO polls, 128

Elections, 11–12, 16, 19–21, 31–32, 39, 170–71, 176

Elites, political: public opinion followed by, 18–23 *passim*, 29; during honeymoon period, 29, 31, 37–38, 39; and rally phenomenon, 55–56, 63–78 *passim*, 151, 166, 169–70; defined, 64–65; and economic performance, 98; and salience of, 112; and position issues, 116–17; and standards of performance evaluation, 120–21; information integration model and, 164; and proposal news, 166–67, 169; and manipulation of news, 172. *See also* Congress; Opinion leaders; Presidents

Employment: presidential popularity and, 91. *See also* Unemployment

Erbring, L., 112

Evaluation: salience in, 106–13; standards for, 113–21; information integration model of, 126–67; performance, 168–76. *See also* Opinion formation

"Exploitable divisions" in the public, 173–75. *See also* Partisan effects

Feldman, S., 107

Fenno, R., 170n

Ferejohn, John, 173

Fleisher, R., 21–22

Ford, Gerald: approval ratings of, 19, 34, 37, 39, 58, 61, 103n; Nixon pardon by, 22, 39–40, 140; honeymoon period of, 34–43 *passim*; and rally phenomenon, 56n, 58, 61, 67; popularity of over time, 87n, 88f; AIPO polls and, 128; information integration model and, 133–52 *passim*, 164

Foreign aid, 8

Foreign policy: under Bush, 7, 8–9; economic, 8, 141; public opinion affecting, 23; during honeymoon period, 33–36; and rally phenomenon, 45–78 *passim*, 147–48, 165, 169–70; information integration model and, 134–38 *passim*, 148–49. *See also* Military developments

"Frustration of power," 141

Fulbright, James William, 69

Gallup Polls, 3, 10–15 *passim*, 19, 27, 127–29; question asked by, 16n, 50, 127; in honeymoon period, 32–43 *passim*; and rally phenomenon, 54ff, 62, 74; information integration model and, 127–29, 142–43

Germany, 7f

Goldenberg, E. N., 112

Goldwater, Barry, 69, 117n

Gorbachev, Mikhail, 74–75

Grenada invasion (1983), 45, 74

Grossman, M., 157

Gross National Product (GNP), federal spending in, 91

Haig, Alexander, 72

Haight, Timothy, 126–33n *passim*, 142, 144, 164

Hersgaard, M., 172n

Hibbs, Douglas, 92–93, 105, 116n

Honeymoon period, 23, 27–44, 99n; Carter's, 12–13, 35–42 *passim*, 160–66 *passim*; Reagan's, 14, 27–28, 32–37 *passim*, 43–44, 160, 166; in second terms, 31–37 *passim*; Ford's, 34–43 *passim*; and rally phenomenon, 49; presidential popularity after, 81–82; standards for evaluation in, 119; information integration model and, 132, 142f

Iceland Summit, 45

Ideology, and standards of performance evaluation, 117–21 *passim*

"Implacability," of special-interest hostility, 88–89

Impression formation, 168–69. *See also* Opinion formation

Income growth rates, and presidential popularity, 92

Independents (party), and economic performance, 92

Inertia, in opinion formation, 122–26, 164–72 *passim*

Inflation, 8, 92–95 *passim*, 99–102, 124; as valence issue, 114, 116n; information integration model and, 136f, 158–65 *passim*

Information integration model, 126–32, 168n; dependent variable and, 127–29; independent variables and, 129–32; and support for presidents Kennedy through Ford, 133–45; and support for presidents Carter and Reagan, 146–67

Information processing, 122–67 *passim. See also* Information integration model; Opinion formation

Innovation, public response to, 171–72

International relations, *see* Crises; Foreign policy

Iran-Contra affair (1986), 45, 54–56, 75–76, 170ff

Iran hostage crisis: rally phenomenon with, 13–14, 45, 49, 62f, 70–76 *passim*, 147–48, 151; information integration model and, 147–48, 151, 158

Israel, 8

"Issue partisans," and popularity over time, 89

Issues: position, 114–21 *passim*, 125; valence, 114–15, 116, 121, 124; single, 120

Iyengar, Shanto, 111n, 112

Johnson, Lyndon B., 19; honeymoon period of, 32–41 *passim*; and rally phenomenon, 51f, 57, 61–62, 67, 71; popularity of over time, 87f; economic performance and, 94, 99, 101; AIPO polls and, 128; information integration model and, 130n, 134–52 *passim*, 164; partisan subgroup evaluation of, 174

KAL-007, 45, 73

Keene, Karlyn, 45

Kennedy, Edward, 12, 72–73, 76

Kennedy, John F., 19; honeymoon period of, 34–39 *passim*; and rally phenomenon, 57, 62, 68–69, 70; popularity of over time, 88; economic performance and, 95, 99, 101f; information integration model and, 133–52 *passim*, 164; partisan subgroup evaluation of, 174

Kernell, Samuel H., 47–52 *passim*, 56n, 60–61, 87n, 126

Khrushchev, Nikita, 67f

Kiewiet, D. R., 108

Kinder, Donald R., 108, 111n, 118n

Kissinger, Henry, 67

Kline, E., 118n

Korean War, 48f

Kraft, Joseph, 76

Kramer, G. H., 108n

Krock, Arthur, 69

Kumar, M., 157

"Lagged approval" variable, 158

"Lagged cumulative news ratio" variable, 158, 160

"Lag structure," 124

Lane, R., 117–18

Laos, 61

Latin America, 7f

Lebanon, 48, 62f, 74

Lee, Jong R., 47, 53–54

Lewis, Anthony, 76

Lippmann, Walter, 17, 76

Lodge, M., 168n

MacKuen, M., 111

Manipulation, of news, 172

Mass opinion, *see* Public opinion

Mayaguez incident (1975), 61, 62–63, 67, 76f

McGraw, K. M., 168n

Media, 171; on economic performance, 98; and salience, 107–13 *passim*; information integration model and, 142, 144, 165; presidential discretionary television, 142, 144; and response to unmediated outcomes, 165, 169. *See also* News

Meese, Edwin, 76

Military developments: and rally phenomenon, 48–49, 56–61 *passim. See also* War

Military power, information integration model and, 141

Miller, A. H., 112

Monroe, K. R., 92n, 124

Morse, Wayne, 70

Mueller, John E., 46n–56 *passim*, 60–61, 77, 86–90 *passim*, 104, 120

National Election Study (NES), 12n, 16n, 55

NATO, 7f

NBC (network), 72, 110n

Neuman, W. R., 111n–12n

Neustadt, Richard, 17, 21, 115–16

News, 4, 9, 169–70, 175–76; interpretation in, 4, 9; and Bush, 8, 10; during honeymoon period, 29–30, 43; and rally phenomenon, 55, 64–77 *passim*, 169–70; and dynamics of presidential popularity, 104–32, 169; and salience, 108–13; editorial practice and, 109–12; and presidential performance evaluation, 116–21 *passim*; information-processing of, 122–67 *passim*; in information integration model, 126–67 *passim*; and presidential proposals, 132–37 *passim*, 157–58, 159, 164–69 *passim*; from Kennedy through Ford, 133–45; under Carter and Reagan, 146–67; presidential manipulation of, 172

"News ratio," *see* Cumulative News Ratio

Newsweek, 27

New York *Times*, 55, 68–77 *passim*, 130; CBS/New York *Times* Poll, 16n, 55, 128

Nicaragua, 7. *See also* Iran-Contra affair

Nie, Norman, 117n–18n

Nisbett, R., 122–23

Nixon, Richard M., 4; pardon of, 22, 39–40, 140; honeymoon period of, 32–42 *passim*; and rally phenomenon, 56n, 57, 62; and Bay of Pigs, 69; popularity of over time, 87ff; economic performance and, 102, 103n; AIPO polls under, 128; information integration model and, 130n, 134–52 *passim*, 164; partisan subgroup evaluation of, 174

Noriega government, 7, 9

Novak, Robert, 76

Occupation groups, and economic performance, 92–93

O'Neill, Thomas, 74

OPEC shock, 138
Opinion formation, 9–10, 23–25, 168–76; politicization of, 4, 117; importance of, 15; in honeymoon period, 33–36; and rally phenomenon, 46, 54; salience in, 54, 106–13; over time, 83–90; standards for performance evaluation in, 113–21; "morselized," 117–18; dynamic and inertial components in, 122–26, 164–72 *passim*; information integration model of, 126–67. *See also* Popularity
Opinion leaders, 4, 9–10, 169–70; defined, 64–65; and domestic crises, 47–48; and international crises, 55–56, 63–67; and rally phenomenon, 55–56, 63–78 *passim*, 166, 169–70; and proposal news, 166–67. *See also* Elites, political; News
Opinion polls, *see* Polls, opinion
Ortega, Daniel, 7
Ostrom, C. W., 114n, 127n
Outcomes, 127, 132–38 *passim*, 167–73 *passim*; economic, 91–105 *passim*; political vs. policy, 119–21; standards for evaluating, 120–21; good/bad/neutral news of, 131–32, 137–66 *passim*; unmediated, 165, 169; of innovation, 171–72

Page, Benjamin, I., 126, 130n
Paldam, M., 92n
Panama, 7, 9

Paris Summit (1960), 59, 67–68
Participant model, and economy, 96, 97–98
Partisan effects, 174–75; after crises of confidence, 40–43 *passim*; and rally phenomenon, 63–77 *passim*, 170, 174; and economic performance, 92–95 *passim*, 99–105n, 161; and standards of performance evaluation, 118–21 *passim*; information integration model and, 161, 164. *See also* Democrats; Republicans
Patriotism, and rally phenomenon, 46, 53–54, 63–66 *passim*, 77
Peffley, M., 105n
Personal life, president's, 113
Policy, *see* Domestic policy; Foreign policy
"Policy proposal" variable, 132, 157–58, 164. *See also* Proposal news
Politics: and news interpretations, 4; democratic, 17–18, 168–76; salience to, 54, 106–13; and popularity over time, 83–88 *passim*; and economic performance, 97–98, 105; and personal problems, 107–8; "vicarious," 108–9; lay theories of, 123–24. *See also* Elites, political
Polls, opinion, 18–19
Polsby, Nelson, 52
Popularity, 3–26 *passim*; explanations of, 24–26, 81–82; economic variables in, 50, 51–52, 91–108 *passim*, 124; variables in (overview), 50–

56; time variable in, 51, 83–90, 104; after honeymoon, 81–82; news and dynamics of, 104–32; salience of evaluation in, 106–13; standards for evaluation in, 113–21; dynamic and inertial components in, 122–26, 164–72 *passim*; information integration model of, 126–67; democracy and, 168–76. *See also* Approval ratings; Elections; Honeymoon period; Rally phenomenon

Position issues, 114–21 *passim*, 125

Presidents: public opinion important to, 15–26 *passim*; legitimacy of, 29; at focus of national politics, 115–16; dynamic and inertial components in support for, 122–26, 164–72 *passim*; direct media access of, 142, 144; two-term limit on, 170n–71n. *See also* Popularity *and individual presidents by name*

Presser, S., 86n

Principal/agent model, 172–73

Proposal news, 132–37 *passim*, 157–58, 159, 164–69 *passim*

Psychology, cognitive, 122–25

Public opinion: theory of, 4–5; importance of, to political elites, 15–26 *passim*; and elections, 16; in democracy, 17–18, 168–76; measuring, 18–19; dynamics of, 23–25, 122–26; crises of confidence in, 40–43; and rally phenomenon, 50–56; and economic

performance, 96–103; sociotropic, 109n–14 *passim*; egocentric, 113; inertia in, 122–26, 164–72 *passim*; information integration model of, 126–67. *See also* Opinion formation; Popularity

Public Opinion (magazine), 45

Public support, *see* Popularity

Pueblo incident (1968), 61–62, 63, 67, 71

Rally phenomenon, 33, 44–81 *passim*; with Carter, 13–14, 45, 56n, 58, 62, 70–77 *passim*, 147–48, 151; criteria for, 47–50, 60–61; as independent variable, 50–52; as dependent variable, 53–56; and opinion leaders, 55–56, 63–78 *passim*, 166, 169–70; data on, 56–63; partisan effects and, 63–77 *passim*, 170, 174; information integration model and, 147–48, 151, 165–66

Reagan, Ronald: approval ratings of, 10–15 *passim*, 19, 27f, 32–37 *passim*, 43–44, 58, 73–75, 102f, 146–47, 159–66 *passim*; AIPO polls and, 14, 27–28, 32–37 *passim*, 43–44, 129, 160, 166; assassination attempt on, 27–28, 43–44, 147, 166; and rally phenomenon, 55–56, 58, 73–76; popularity of over time, 83, 88f, 104; economic performance and, 95, 102, 103n, 105n, 162–65 *passim*, 169, 174; information integration model and, 135, 140,

146–67; manipulation of news attempted by, 172n
Recessions, 105n, 108, 137, 174
Republicans, 41–43, 69–75 *passim*, 92–95 *passim*, 99–103 *passim*, 161
Reston, James, 77
Results, *see* Outcomes
Reykjavik Summit (1986), 59, 74–75
Rivers, H. D., 21–22, 159
Rockefeller, Nelson, 69
Roosevelt, F. D., 172n
Rose, N. L., 21–22
Ross, L., 122–23
Rusk, Dean, 69

Sadat, Anwar, 13
Salience, in performance evaluation, 54, 106–13
Schlozman, K. L., 107–8
Schroeder, Patricia, 153
Shapiro, Catherine R., 47, 54–55
Short-term surges variable, in presidential popularity, 51–52
Shultz, George, 75
Sigelman, L., 16n, 20n, 46, 71n
Simon, D. M., 114n, 127n
"Single-issue" standard, 120
Sniderman, P., 107
"Sociotropic" judgments, 109n–14 *passim*
South Africa, 7
Soviet Union, 7f, 49, 56, 67–68, 77, 135, 141
Spectator model, and economy, 96–98
Spending, federal, 91
Sputnik I, 49
"Stagflation," 137
Stevenson, Adlai, 68

Stimson, J. A., 33, 51, 83–90 *passim*, 104
Stokes, Donald, 114f
Stroh, P., 168n
Summit meetings, and rally phenomenon, 13, 49, 56, 58–60, 67–68, 74–75, 147–48
Support, public, *see* Popularity

"Talk" variable, 132. *See also* Proposal news
Technological developments, and rally phenomenon, 49
Television, *see* Media
Television News Abstracts and Index (Vanderbilt University), 130
Thailand, 61
Time variable, in presidential popularity, 51, 83–90, 104
Transfer payments, federal, 91
Truman, Harry S., 19, 30n, 57, 62, 89, 94, 99, 101f, 128
Truman Doctrine, 49

U-2 incident (1960), 49, 59, 62, 67–68, 71, 76
Unemployment, 8, 91–103 *passim*, 107–8, 114, 116n, 124, 136, 158–65 *passim*
United Nations, 68f
Unna, Warren, 67

Valence issues, 114–15, 116, 121, 124
Vanderbilt University, 130
Verba, S., 107–8
Vietnam War, 22, 40–43, 49, 51, 62f, 113, 128, 134–41 *passim*, 153, 174
Voting, *see* Elections

Waltz, K., 46, 63

War: Korean, 48f; and rally phenomenon, 49, 56, 58–59; as a
variable in presidential popularity, 50. *See also* Vietnam
War

Washington *Post*, 67–68, 72–77
passim

Watergate, 22, 88, 102, 105; and
honeymoon, 40, 42–43; and
salience, 113; information integration model and, 128,
134–40 *passim*, 151, 153; partisan subgroups and, 174

Weatherford, M. S., 118n

White-collar workers, and economic performance, 92–93

Williams, J. T., 105n

Library of Congress Cataloging-in-Publication Data

Brody, Richard A.
   Assessing the president: the media, elite opinion, and public
support / Richard A. Brody.
   p.   cm.
   Includes bibliographical references and index.
   ISBN 0-8047-1907-1 (cloth): ISBN 0-8047-2096-7 (pbk.)
   1. Presidents—United States—Public opinion.   2. Public
opinion—United States.   3. Press—United States.   I. Title.
JK518.B77   1991
353.03'5—dc20   90-24711
                                                       CIP

⊗ This book is printed on acid-free paper.